Carsten Rasch   / Mei - Fang Lin

—

DICTIONARY OF LAW

ENGLISH - CHINESE

Carsten Rasch / Mei - Fang Lin

-

DICTIONARY OF LAW

ENGLISH - CHINESE

Herstellung und Verlag:
BoD - Books on Demand, Norderstedt
ISBN 978-3-7347-6183-6

The Dictionary of Law with over 5,000 words covers the basic legal terminology used in the English language with equivalent terms from China.

The English - Chinese vocabulary provides assistance for translation and understanding of legal texts in English and Chinese context.

A simple defining style and a clear colour layout ensure the dictionary text is accessible and easy to use.

This portable and affordable dictionary of Law is an essential reference tool for all college and university students who need practical advice and tips to tackle their studies.

Carsten Rasch and Mei - Fang Lin

# A

- ab initio   自始
- ab intestate   无遗嘱的继承,无遗嘱死亡时
- abandonment   放弃,遗弃,委付
- abandonment of action   放弃诉讼
- abandonment of claim   放弃索赔
- abandonment of right   放弃权力
- to abate   降低、减少、排除
- abatement   取消,减除,减额
- abatement of action   中止诉讼,撤销诉讼
- abatement of legacy   全部或部分遗产的中止承受
- to abduct   拐騙、誘拐
- abduction   诱拐,劫持,绑架
- abductor   诱拐者
- abet   教唆,煽動
- abetment   教唆犯罪,助人犯罪
- able-bodied   身心健康

- abnormal   反常,变态
- abnormality of mind   精神失常
- abode   住所,常住地
- abolition   废除,取消
- abominable crime   可鄙的罪行
- abominable   可鄙,可憎,可恶
- abortion   堕胎
- above par   高於票面值
- above reproach   无可指责
- abrogation   取消,撤销,废除
- abscond   潛逃、逃跑
- absconder   潛逃者
- absconding debtor   逃债者
- absence of consideration   缺乏约因
- absence without leave   擅自不出庭
- absenteeism   缺勤
- absolute   无条件的,完全的
- absolute advantage   絕對優勢
- absolute decree   最后判决,最终裁定
- absolute discretion   绝对酌情决定权

- absolute liability 绝对责任,绝对赔偿责任
- absolute title 绝对所有权
- absolve 宣告无罪,免除
- absorption costing 全部成本法,全面成本法
- abstain 弃权,戒除
- abstain from pleading 放弃申辩
- abstention 弃权
- abstinence of drug 戒除毒瘾
- abstract 摘要
- abstract of title 产业契据摘要,地契摘要
- abuse 滥用,辱骂,虐待,弊端
- abuse (office) 濫用職權
- abuse (people) 虐待、辱罵
- abuse (power) 濫用權力
- abuse of distress 濫用扣押物
- abuse of process 滥用诉讼程序
- accelerated depreciation 加速折舊
- acceptance 承兌,承兌票據,承諾
- acceptance of bill of exchange 匯票承兌
- acceptance of bribes 受賄

- acceptance of service    接受传票
- accepted draft (bill)    已承兌匯票(票據)
- accepting bank    承兌银行
- acceptor    承兌人
- access    探视儿女权,进入权,接近途径
- accessory after the fact    事後從犯
- accessory before the fact    事前從犯
- accessory during the fact    作案從犯
- accessory    从犯,同谋,附属物,附件
- accident    意外事件,事故
- accident insurance    意外保險
- accidental homicide    意外杀人,非故意杀人
- accommodation    调解,通融,住宿
- accomplice    共犯,同谋
- accord and satisfaction    和解与清償
- according to law    按照法律、依照法律
- accost    勾引(妓女等),引诱,搭讪
- account    帳,帳戶,科目,客帳
- account executive    客戶主任,戶口主任
- account form    帳戶式

- account number    帳号
- account payee only    只可轉帳
- account sales    承銷清單,銷貨清單
- accountability    責任承擔
- accountable    有说明义务的,负有责任的,可解释的
- accountant general    主計署署长,总会计师
- accountant    會計人員,會計主任,會計師
- accounting assumption    會計假設
- accounting base    會計基礎
- accounting concept    會計觀念,會計概念
- accounting control    會計牽制,會計統制
- accounting convention    會計慣例
- accounting cycle    會計循環
- accounting department    会记部
- accounting element    會計要素
- accounting entity    會計個體
- accounting equation    會計等式
- accounting error    會計錯誤
- accounting framework    會計架構
- accounting identity    會計等式

- accounting information system　會計資訊系統
- accounting period　會計期間,會計結算期
- accounting policy　會計政策
- accounting principles　会计准则
- accounting procedure　會計程序
- accounting rate of return　會計報酬率
- accounting ratio　會計比率
- accounting record　會計記錄
- accounting report　會計報告
- accounting software　會計軟體
- accounting standards　會計準則
- accounting statement　會計報表
- accounting system　會計制度
- accounting theory　會計理論
- accounting transaction　會計事項,帳務交易
- accounting year　會計年度
- accounting bookkeeping　簿记、会记
- accounting reporting　财务报告制度
- accounts　科目
- accounts payable　應付帳款

- accounts payable turnover   應付帳款周轉率
- accounts receivable   應收帳款
- accounts receivable turnover   應收帳款周轉率
- accretion   財产的自然增值,添加物
- accrual accounting   應計會計
- accrual concept   應計觀念
- accrual date   應收日,應付日
- accruals   應計項目
- accrued asset   應計資產
- accrued basis   應計基礎
- accrued depreciation   應計折舊
- accrued dividend   應計股息
- accrued expense   應計費用
- accrued income   應計收益
- accrued item   應計項目
- accumulated deficit   累计亏损
- accumulated depreciation   累積折舊,折舊準備
- accumulated dividend   累積股息
- accumulated fund   累積基金
- accusation   控告,起诉,告发,谴责

- accusatory instrument　控告文書
- to accuse　控诉,控告,指责
- accused　被告
- achievement test　成就測驗
- acid test ratio　酸性測驗比率
- acid test　酸性測驗
- acknowledgment of debt　承認負債
- acknowledgment of natural child　私生子女的认领
- acknowledgment　承认,收讫
- acquiescence　默许,默认
- acquired right(s)　既得权利
- acquisition　征用,收购,取得
- acquisition accounting　購買會計法,收購會計法
- acquisition cost　取得成本,購入成本,購置成本
- acquisition of land　土地征用
- acquit　宣告無罪
- acquittal　宣告无罪,清偿债务,履行职责
- acquitted of a charge　无罪释放
- act　法令,行为
- act of Congress　國會法案

- act of God　不可抗力、天災
- act of indemnity　特赦行為
- act of law　法律行為,法律作用,法律效力
- action　起訴,行為,行動,訴訟
- active partner　活躍合夥人,積極參與業務的合夥人
- activity ratio　實際作業與預算比率
- activity　活动
- actuarial report　精算报表
- actus reus　被告的行為,犯罪的行為
- ad hoc committee　臨時委員會,專責委員會
- ad hoc　特別,特定,专门,临时
- ad idem　一致,意见相同
- ad infinitum　无限
- ad litem　诉讼的,为诉讼
- ad valorem duty　從價稅,按值計稅
- ad valorem　按值纳税,按值征税,从价税
- added value　增值額,增加值
- addendum　附录,补遗,附件
- to adduce　引证,提出,援引
- to adjourn　延期

- adjudicate 判决
- adjudication 裁决,判决,宣判,宣告
- adjudication of bankruptcy 宣告破产
- adjudication of delinquency 罪判决為青少年犯
- adjusting entry 調整分錄
- adjusting event 調整事項
- adjustment 調整
- administer an oath 監誓
- administration bond 遗产管理保证书
- administration of an estate 遗产管理
- administration of justice 司法,执法
- administration of property 财产管理
- administration 遗产管理,行政,政府
- administrative overhead 行政費用
- administrator 遗产管理人
- administratrix 女遗产管理人
- admissibility in evidence 可接受作為证据
- admissibility 可入為証
- admissible evidence 可接納的證據
- admission [into custody or incarceration] 收押

- admission [statement or confession]　承認
- admission of fact　事实的招认
- admission of new partner　新合夥人加入,新入夥
- admission　供认、招认 供認、招認
- admitted into evidence　接收為證據
- admonition　告诫,警告
- adolescence　青春期
- to adopt　采用,采取,正式通过
- adoption　收養、領養、認養,採用、接納
- adoptive　采用的
- adulteration　伪造,掺假
- adulterer　奸夫
- adulteress　奸妇
- adultery　通奸
- advance　預付,預付款項
- advancement　晉升
- adverse　相反的,逆的,不利的
- adverse verdict　不利的裁决
- adverse witness　不利证人,敌对证人
- advertising　廣告

- advertising agency   廣告公司,廣告代理商
- advertising appeal   廣告訴求
- advertising media   廣告媒介
- advice note   交貨通知書
- advice, debate   咨询、协商
- advisement of rights   權利告誡
- advisory body   顾问团体
- advisory support   諮詢上的支援,顧問支援
- advocate   辯護人
- to advocate   辯護,倡導
- affairs   事务,事态,私通事件
- affiant   宣誓人、立誓人
- affidavit   宣誓书
- affidavit of means   有能力償债证明的宣誓书
- affiliated company   附属公司
- affirm   確認（上訴院）維持原判
- affirmation   誓言,证实 , 声明
- affray   打架,闹事,在公共场所互殴
- aforethought   预谋的
- aforethought malice   预怀恶意

- aftercare 假釋
- after-sales service 售後服務
- age for/of marriage 结婚年龄
- age of majority 成年,法定年龄,法定成年人年龄
- agency 代办处、代理处
- agency business 托售、代销
- agency fee / commission fee 手续费
- agent 代理人
- agent ad litem 诉讼代理人
- agent provocateur 坐探,密探
- aggravated 加重的
- aggravated arson 惡性縱火
- aggravated assault 惡性攻擊
- aggravated circumstances 增加嚴重性的情節
- aggravated criminal contempt 惡性藐視法庭
- aggravated harassment 惡性騷擾
- aggravated sexual abuse 惡性性虐待
- aggravated theft 惡性盜竊
- aggravating circumstances 可加重罪行的情況
- aggravation 加重,严重

- aggravation of penalty  刑罰加重,加重刑罰
- aggregate depreciation  累計折舊
- aggrieved  受害的,受委屈的,悲痛的
- aggrieved party  被害人(方),受害人(方)
- aging problem  高齡問題,老齡化問題
- aging schedule for doubtful debts  呆帳帳齡分析表
- agreement  合约,合同,协议,协定,协同行为
- to aid and abet  協謀、教唆、
- aiding prostitution  協助賣淫
- aids to trade  貿易輔助服務
- air freight  航空貨運費
- air transport  航空運輸
- air waybill  空運提貨單,空運提單
- alias  別名、化名、假名
- alibi  不在犯罪现场,以不在犯罪现场为辩护理由
- alien  外僑、僑民
- alimony  生活费,赡养费
- allegation  指控,声称,指责
- to allege  聲稱
- alleged cause  声称的事由,引证原因,陈诉的理由

- alleged thief    被指稱爲竊賊的人
- allied company    联号,联合公司
- allocate    分配
- allocution    認罪供詞、自白供詞
- allotment    分配數,分配額
- allowance    折讓,津貼,免稅額
- allowance for doubtful accounts    呆帳準備
- alteration of capital    股本更改
- alternative    方案,備選
- amalgamation    合併
- amend    修改
- amended pleading(s)    修正的诉状
- amendment    修改
- amendment of writ    令狀的修正
- amends    赔偿,赔罪
- amentia    智力缺陷,精神错乱
- amicus curiae    法庭之友
- ammunition    彈葯
- amnesia    健忘,记忆缺失
- amnesty    特赦,赦免

- amortization　攤銷
- amount of annuity　年金金額
- analysis　分析
- anchorage　抛锚地
- ancillary　辅助的,附属的
- animal cruelty　虐畜罪
- annex　附录,附件,附属建筑物
- annexation　附加物,并吞,侵吞
- annual　年度的
- annual accounts　年度结算,年度帐
- annual audit　周年核數
- annual audit　年度审计
- annual financial statements　年度会计报表
- annual general meeting　年度会议
- annual leave　年假
- annual report　年報
- annual return　周年回報,年報,年收益率
- annual value　年值
- annuity　年金
- annuity depreciation method　年金折舊法

- annulment   废止,废除,取消,无效
- annulment of marriage   婚姻无效
- antecedents   前例,先例,前事,祖先
- ante-dated cheque   倒填日期的支票
- anticipated profit   預期利潤
- anticompetitive practices   防止競爭措施
- anti-corruption   反贪污
- antitrust act   反托拉斯法案、發信托案
- apparent   明显的
- to appeal   上訴
- appeal against conviction   不服定罪的上诉
- appeal against sentence   不服判刑的上诉
- appeal allowed   上诉获准
- appeal dismissed   上诉驳回
- appeal tribunal   上诉法庭
- appearance   出庭
- appellant   上訴人
- appellate court   上訴法庭
- appellate jurisdiction   上诉裁判权
- applicability   可適應性

- applicant 申请人
- application 申请
- application of fund 資金運用
- appoint 指定、委派、委任
- appointment 委任,指定,任命,任用,选派,职位
- apportionment 分攤
- apportionment of profit 盈利分配
- apportionment of shares 股票分配
- appraisal 估價
- appraise 評定
- appreciation 增值,升值
- appreciation tax 土地增值稅
- apprehend [a person] 逮捕某人
- apprehension 逮捕,拘押,忧虑,恐惧
- apprehension of injury 伤害之虑
- apprehension of violence 暴力之虑
- apprenticeship 學徒訓練,學徒制
- appropriation 撥用,分配
- approval 批准,核准,认可
- approval, consent 认可、同意

- approved school    少年犯教养院,收容所
- aptitude test    性向測驗,能向測驗
- arbitrage    套利,套息,套戥
- arbitral award    仲裁裁决
- arbitrary    武断的,任意的,擅自的
- arbitration    仲裁,公断
- arbitration tribunal    仲裁法庭
- arbitrator    仲裁人,公断人
- argumentative question    爭論性的問題
- argument    爭辯、辯論
- arm of the law    法律的權利
- armed felony    持械重罪
- armed robbery    持械搶劫
- arm's length transaction    正當交易
- arms offences act    枪械罪行法令
- arraign    传讯,提审,控告
- arraignment    提審、提訊、提堂、過堂
- arraignment hearing    提訊聽證
- arrears    積欠
- arrest    拘捕,逮捕

- arrest on suspicion　因有疑而被捕
- arrest procedure　逮捕程序
- arrest record　逮捕記錄
- arrest warrant　逮捕証、通緝令
- arrestable offence　可被拘捕的罪行
- arresting officer　執行逮捕的警員
- arsenal　彈藥庫、槍械庫
- arson　縱火罪
- ascertain　確定、查明
- aspersion　中傷、誹謗
- assailant　攻擊者
- assassin　刺客、暗殺兇手
- assassination　暗杀,行刺
- assault　袭击,殴打,凌辱,侮辱
- assault and battery　毆打罪、傷害人身罪
- assembling　裝配
- assembly line　裝配線
- assent　认可,批准
- assertion　断言,宣称,维护,坚持
- assertive evidence　有力证据

- assessment 评价,评估,评定
- assessment basis 评估基础
- assessment of damages 评估损失赔偿额
- assessor 估价财产的人,审查税款的人,技术顾问
- assess 估價
- asset 資產
- asset turnover 資產周轉率
- assets and liabilities 资产与负债
- assign 转让,委派
- assigned counsel 公設辯護人
- assignee 受让人,受托者
- assigner 转让者,委托者
- assignment 转让,委派,委托
- assignment cost 轉讓成本
- assignment of responsibility 職責之指派
- assistant Corporation Counsel (ACC) 助理政府律师
- assistant District Attorney (ADA) 助理地區檢察官
- associated company 联营公司,联号
- association 协会,社团,公会
- assumption 估计、猜测、假设

- assumption of duty  就任,就職,上任
- asylum  避难,庇护,收容所
- at cost  按成本
- at large  逍遥法外,未被捕
- at market  按市值
- at one's own risk  自己负责,自担风险
- at par  照票面价值
- at sight  見票即付
- at variance  不一致
- atrocity  暴行
- attaché  使馆馆员,外交使节随员
- attachment  扣押财产,逮捕,附属品
- attachment of debt  债款扣押
- attachment of earnings  扣发工资
- attachment order  扣押令
- attempt  企圖
- attempted crime  犯罪未遂
- attempted murder  謀殺未遂
- attest  證明
- attestation  证明,证实,证据,宣誓

- attesting witness  作证人,见证人,证明人
- attorney  受权人,受任人,代理人,(美)律师
- attorney-client privilege  律師與當事人的守密權
- attributable profit  可歸屬利潤
- auction  拍卖
- auction by government  由政府拍卖
- audience  接见,听讼
- audit  审计,查帐,审核
- audit committee  核數委員會,審計委員會
- audit of financial statements  财务报表审计
- audit of statutory accounts  法定财务报表审计
- audit opinion  审计意见、审计报告
- audit report  审计报告
- audit the books  查帐
- auditor  审计师,查帐人
- auditor's remuneration  核數師酬金
- auditor's report  核數師報告
- authenticate  鑒定、認證
- authentication of documents  文件的鉴定
- authentication  鉴定,证实,认证

- authorised capital    法定資本,註冊股本
- authoritarian    獨裁,專制
- authority    权力,权威,典据,判决例
- authorization    授权,认可
- authorization power of attorney 委托，法律授权书
- authorize    授权,委任,核准,认可
- authorized by law    经法律许可
- authorized capital    核定资本
- auto theft    偷汽車
- autocratic leadership    獨裁式領導,專制式領導
- automatic credit transfer    自動轉帳收款
- automatic pistol    自動手槍
- automobile homicide    車禍殺人
- autonomous work group    自治工作小組
- autonomy    自主,自治權
- autopay    自動轉帳支付
- autopsy    驗屍、屍體剖檢
- availability    可用性,有效性,效力
- available cash    備用現金
- aver    证明,断言

- average clause　受保範圍,損失條款
- average collection period　平均收帳期
- average cost　平均成本
- average stock　平均存貨
- averment　事实的陈述
- avoidable cost　可避免成本
- avoidable risk　可避免之風險
- avoidance of tax　避稅
- avow　招認、承認
- await sentence　等待判刑
- await trial　候審
- award and punishment　獎懲
- award　判决,判定,判给,授与

# B

- backup　後援、後備
- backward integration　後向合併
- bad debt　呆帳
- badge (of a police officer)　徽章
- bail　保釋金
- bail bond　保释保证书
- bail bondsman　保釋代理人
- bail forfeiture　保釋金沒收
- bail jumping　棄保潛逃、保釋中逃跑、逃跑
- to bail out　保釋，保釋外出
- bail revocation　撤銷保釋
- bailee　受託人
- bailey　法庭
- bailiff　法警、法庭執行官
- bailment　寄託,委託
- bailor　保释人,委托保管人,财物寄托人

- balance   收付平衡,收付差额,余额
- balance of payments   國際收支差額,國際收支平衡
- balance of trade   貿易差額
- balance sheet date, closing date   资产负债表日
- balance sheet total, total assets   总资产
- balance unclaimed   未提取的存款,余款
- balancing day adjustment   期末調整
- balancing off account   結帳,帳戶結平
- ballistics   彈道學
- ban   禁止、禁令、取締
- bandit   歹徒,盜匪
- banishment   驱逐出境,逐放
- banish   流放、驅逐
- bank   银行
- bank acceptance   銀行承兌
- bank account   銀行帳戶
- bank bill   銀行匯票
- bank book   銀行存折
- bank charge   銀行手續費
- bank clearing   银行票据交换

- bank code number　银行代号
- bank credit　银行信贷
- bank deposit　银行存款
- bank discount　銀行貼現息
- bank draft　銀行匯票
- bank interest rate　銀行利率
- bank interest　銀行利息
- bank levy　银行税
- bank loan　銀行貸款
- bank lodgement　尚未記錄存款
- bank money　银行票据
- bank note　钞票
- bank overdraft　銀行透支
- bank rate　银行贴现率,银行利率
- bank reconciliation statement　銀行往來調節表
- bank run　银行挤提
- bank statement　銀行報告,銀行結單
- bank transfer　银行转帐
- bank's orders　本票
- banker　银行家,(赌博)发牌人

- banker's acceptance 銀行承兌票據
- banknote 銀行紙幣
- bankrupt 破产者
- bankruptcy notice 破产通知书,催还债款通知
- bankruptcy petition 申请宣布破产的请求书
- bar 法庭的围栏,律师席,律师业,停止诉讼的申请
- barricade 臨時防禦、障礙物
- barter 以貨易貨,以物易物
- base stock 基本存貨量
- basic credit line 贷款限额
- basic need 基本需要
- basic salary 底薪
- basis of preparation 编制基础
- batch processing 成批處理,整批處理
- bear 看淡股市者,淡友
- bear market 熊市,淡市
- bear witness 作证,证明
- bearer 持信人,持票人,持有人
- bearer bond 息票債券,不記名債券
- bearer cheque 來人支票,不記名支票

- bearer share　無記名股票,不記名股票
- bearing in mind　顧及,記着
- bearing scrapers　三角锉
- befouling water　污染水源
- behavior　品性、行爲
- below par　低於票面值
- bench　法官席、法官
- bench conference　法席前會議
- bench trail　法官（無陪審團）審訊
- bench warrant　法庭傳票
- benefactor　捐贈人,施主,恩人
- beneficiary　受益人,信托收益人,收款人
- benefit　利益,权益,津贴,补助金，福利
- benefit management　福利管理
- benefit of doubt　假定某人无罪
- benefit survey　福利調查
- bequest　动产的遺赠,遗产
- best lending rate　最優惠利率,最優惠貸款利率
- betray　背叛,出卖,泄露
- betrayal　背叛,告密,通敌

- betrayer 背叛者,告密者,叛徒
- betroth 订婚,许配
- betterment 不动产增值,地产增值,改善,改良
- betting 打赌,赌博,博彩
- beyond reasonable doubt 理無置疑、無合理懷疑
- beyond suspicion 无可怀疑
- bias 偏见,不公正,先入之见
- bid 出价,投标
- bidder 出价人,投标人
- bigamous marriage 重婚
- bigamy 一夫多妻制,重婚罪
- bilateral agreement 双边协定
- bill (in a legislature) 議案
- bill of exchange 匯票,票據,交易票據
- bill of indictment 刑事起诉讼,刑事起诉书
- bill of lading 提貨單
- bill of particular 訴訟明細書
- Bill of Rights 人權法案、基本權利法案
- bill payable 應付票據
- bill receivable 應收票據

- bill 法案,票据,汇票,帐单,清单,诉状,起诉书
- bind over 責令待審
- binding 有約束力的、附有義務的
- binding agreement 有約束力的協議
- binding effect 约束力,约束效能
- binding force 约束力,拘束力
- binding precedent 有约束力的判例,有约束力的先例
- biological parents 生父母
- birthright 与生俱來的權利
- black market 黑市
- black-listed 列入黑名单
- blackmail 勒索、敲詐、訛詐
- blank cheque 空白支票
- blasphemy 褻瀆,侮辱
- Blood Alcohol Content (BAC) 血液酒精含量 (BAC)
- blood alcohol 血液內的酒精含量
- blood relation 血亲,血缘关系
- blood test 驗血
- bludgeon 杖刑
- blue-collar 蓝领阶级的,工人阶级的

- board member　董事会成员
- board of directors　董事会
- board of directors　董事會,董事局
- bodily harm　身体伤害
- bodily punishment　体罚
- body　身体,团体,正文
- body of deed　契据本文
- body of persons　社团
- body search　搜身
- bona fide claim　善意要求,真诚要求
- bona fide　善意,真诚,信誉
- bond dividend　債券利息,債券股利,債券紅利
- bond interest　債券利息
- bond　公债,债券,契约,盟约,保证金,保证书
- bonded warehouse　保税仓库
- bone of contention　争端,争论的原因
- bonus　紅利,花紅
- bonus issue　發行紅股
- bonus share　紅股,股票股息
- book inventory　帳面存貨

- book of original entry    原始分錄簿,原始計錄簿
- book value    帳面值,帳面成本
- to book    入案、落案
- bookie / bookmaker    賭博（各種比賽）的經濟人
- booking    落案
- bookkeeping cycle    簿記循環
- bookmaking    外圍下注
- boot-legging    走私漏稅,違禁卖酒
- borrowing costs    借款費用
- bought day book    購貨日記簿
- bound    受到約束的
- boycott    杯葛,抵制
- brain drain    人才流失,人才外流
- brain storming    刺激創新,腦力激盪法
- branch    分公司、分行
- brand image    品牌形象,牌子形象
- brand loyalty    對牌子忠誠
- brand    品牌
- brandish a weapon    揮動武器（來威脅）
- breach    破坏,違反,不履行,破裂

- breach of agreement 违反协约
- breach of discipline 破坏纪律,违反纪律
- breach of promise 违约,食言,违背婚约
- breakeven analysis 損益平衡分析,損益兩平分析
- breakeven chart 損益平衡圖,損益兩平圖
- breakeven point 損益平衡點,損益兩平點
- breaking and entering 強行闖入
- bribe 行賄、賄賂
- bribery 賄賂
- brief 摘要書
- bring to justice 繩之以法
- broker 經紀
- brokerage firm 經紀行
- brought down 承上
- brought forward 承前
- budget 預算
- budgetary control 預算控制
- budgeting 預算,編製預算
- budgeting variance 預算差異
- buffer stock 調節存貨,安全存貨

- bulk-breaking　分件
- bulk-buying　大量購買
- bull market　牛市,旺市
- bull　看好股市者,好友
- bullet　子彈頭
- bulletproof vest　防彈背心
- burden (financial)　負担（金融）
- burden of proof　举证责任
- bureaucracy　官僚系統,官僚組織制度
- burglary insurance　盜竊保險
- burglary　盜竊、盜竊罪
- business administration　工商管理
- business behavior　商業行為
- business combination　企业合并
- business communication　商業溝通傳意
- business concept　商業概念
- business corporation　企業公司
- business customer　商業顧客
- business cycle　商業循環,營業循環,營業週期
- business enterprise　企業機構

- business entity concept　企業個體觀念
- business environment　營商環境
- business ethics　商業道德
- business function　商業功能
- business information　商業資訊
- business issue　商業事務
- business license　營業執照
- business management　商業管理
- business market　商業消費市場
- business opportunity　商機
- business organisation　企業組織
- business ownership　企業擁有權
- business plan　商業計畫書
- business registration certificate　商業登記證
- business reply service　商業回郵服務
- business risk　經營風險
- business sector　商界
- business tax　营业税
- business transaction　业务
- business venture　企業

- buy & bust operation　買及拉，買抓行動
- buying power index　購買力指數
- bylaws　規章、規程

# C

- calculating device 計算裝置
- callable bond 可贖回債券
- called-up capital 已催繳股本
- campaign contribution 競選捐獻、競選獻金
- cannabis 大麻、大麻類毒品
- capacitate 使在法律上合格,使具有资格
- capacity 权能,资格,能力,才能,行为能力
- capacity of legacy 遗产继承资格,受遗赠能力
- capacity of marriage 结婚资格
- capacity to consent 法律上的同意能力
- capacity to contract 订约资格,订约能力
- capacity utilisation 产能利用率
- capital 资本,首都,死刑
- capital allowance 投資補貼,資本資產稅務折舊扣減
- capital budgeting 資本預算
- capital contribution 投入资本

- capital crime　死刑罪
- capital donation　資本捐贈
- capital employed　動用資金,動用資本
- capital expenditure　資本支出,資本開支
- capital gain　資本利得,資本增值,資本增益
- capital gearing　資本與負債比率,資金借貸比率
- capital goods　資本物品
- capital increase　增资
- capital intensive　資本密集
- capital investment appraisal　資本投資評估
- capital maintenance　資本保留,資本保全
- capital market　資本市場
- capital offence　死罪,死刑罪,可以处死的罪行
- capital punishment　死刑
- capital reconstruction　資本重組
- capital redemption reserve　贖回資本準備
- capital reduction　資本縮減
- capital reorganization　資本重組
- capital reserve　資本公積金,資金儲備,資本準備
- capital stock　创始资本

- capital structure    資本結構
- capital transfer tax    資本转让税
- capitalisation    資本化,利益資本化
- capitalism    資本主義
- capitalist economy    資本主義經濟
- care    小心,謹慎,注意,照顾,看护,管理
- care order    (少年犯罪法庭等)对儿童的保管令
- careless driving    不小心驾驶
- cargo insurance    貨物保險,貨運險
- carjacking    劫車
- carpool lane    合用車專用道
- carriage forward    運費到付,貨價不包括運費
- carriage inwards    購貨運費
- carriage outwards    銷貨運費
- carriage paid    運費已付,貨價包括運費
- carried down    轉下,結轉下期
- carried forward    延後,結轉下期
- carrier    運貨工具,承運商
- carrying a concealed weapon    攜帶暗器
- carrying cost    貯存成本,存倉成本

- case　訴訟, 案件, 案情, 判例, 事例, 实例, 狀況
- case in chief　主案、控方的證據
- case law　判例法、案例法
- cash　現金
- cash accounting　現金會計
- cash at bank　銀行存款
- cash balance　現金余額
- cash banked　已存入銀行現金
- cash basis　現金基礎
- cash book　現金日記簿, 現金簿
- cash budget　現金預算
- cash discount　現金折扣
- cash dispenser　現金提款機
- cash dividend　現金股息
- cash flow　現金流量
- cash flow statement　現金流量表
- cash forecast　現金預測
- cash in hand　庫存現金, 手頭現金
- cash in transit　在途現金
- cash management　現金管理

- cash over and short    現金尾差,現金溢缺
- cash rebate    現金回扣
- cash sale    現銷,現金銷貨
- cash statement    庫存表,現金報表
- cash with order    訂貨付現
- cashier order    銀行本票,銀行票
- cassation    翻案,取消,廢除
- category method    按類別存貨計價法
- causal    原因的
- causation    因果關係、造事原因
- cause and effect    因果
- cause of action    訴訟原因,案由,訴因
- cause    訴因,案件,訴訟,起因,理由,事業
- causing catastrophe    造成大災難
- caveat    警告、中止訴訟的通知
- caveat against arrest    中止财产扣押的申请
- caveat emptor    購者自慎
- cease and desist    停止、制止
- censorship    审查,检查
- censure    指责,非难,苛评,谴责

- census    人口普查,人口调查,统计
- central tendency    中央傾向,集中趨勢
- centralisation    集中,集中化
- centralised management    中央集權管理
- centre    中心,中央,中心区
- certificate of marriage    结婚证书
- certificate of Origin    產地來源證
- certificate of posting    投寄郵件證明書
- certificate of title    所有权证明书,地契
- certificate of validity    有效证明书
- certificate    证书,执照,证券,股票,单据,凭单
- certified    被證明的、有保證的
- certified copy    经核证副本,核证副本
- cessation    停止,休止,中止,中断
- chain of command    命令線,命令鏈,指揮鏈
- chain of custody    接受監管的次序
- chain store    連鎖商店
- chairman of the board    董事长
- chairman    主席
- challenge    挑战,质问,正式提出反对

- challenge for cause    有原因要求陪審員退席
- challenge of juror    反对某人为陪审员
- chamber    会议室,会议厅,会所
- change of venue    變更審判地點、轉移管轄
- channel of information    資訊管道
- character    特性,性质,特征,性格,品质,人物
- character evidence    人品的证据,品格证据
- charge    控罪
- to charge    控告
- charge of murder    谋杀罪名,控以谋杀罪
- charge to the jury    （法官）對陪審團的指導
- chargeable    可能被控的,应课税的,应付费的
- charges    指控、罪名
- charitable donation    慈善捐款
- charitable organization    慈善機構、慈善組織
- charity drive    慈善活動
- chastisement    惩罚,严惩,责罚,惩戒
- chattel    動產、有形財產
- chattel mortgage    动产抵押
- chattel personal    个人动产

- chattel real     准不动产,准实产
- cheat     欺诈,欺骗行为,骗取,骗子
- check, cheque     支票
- cheque clearance     支票交換
- chief financial controller     財務總經理
- chief justice     首席法官
- chief tenant     包租人,二房东
- child abuse     虐待兒童
- child endangerment     危害兒童
- child labor law     童工法
- child molestation     猥褻兒童
- child neglect     忽視兒童
- child protection order     儿童保护令
- child welfare service     兒童福利服務
- choke     闷死,窒息,说不出话来
- choking     窒息
- choose to remain silent     选择保持缄默
- chop     戳印,官印,商标,图章
- chose     所有物,物,动产
- circuit court     巡迴法庭

- circulating asset　流動資產
- circulating capital　營運資金,周轉資金
- circumstance(s)　情况,环境,形势,事项,事件
- circumstantial　按照情况的,视情况而定的
- circumstantial evidence　间接证据,旁证,情况证据
- citation　援引,引证,引述,引文,引判例为证
- citizen　公民,国民
- citizenship　国籍,公民权,公民资格,公民身份
- civil　民事
- civil action　民事诉讼
- civil case　民事案件,民事诉讼
- civil code　民事法典
- civil court　民事法庭
- civil death　褫夺公权
- civil disobedience　非暴力反抗
- civil enforcement　執行民事法典
- civil jurisdiction　民事司法管辖权,民事审判权
- civil law　民事法
- civil libel　民事诽谤
- civil liberty　公民自由

- civil marriage 世俗结婚
- civil procedure 民事诉讼程序
- civil proceedings 民事诉讼,民事诉讼程序
- civil process 民事诉讼(程序)
- civil responsibility 民事责任
- civil right 公民權利
- civil suit 民事诉讼
- civil trial 民事案件的审讯
- civil wrong 民事过失,民事不法行为
- claim (damages) 索賠
- claim (lost or stolen property) 認領
- claim 要求權
- to claim 聲稱、斷言
- claim in detinue 要求交还非法扣押物
- claim, title 权益,所有权
- claimant 債權人、原告、索賠人
- clandestine 暗中的、秘密的
- clarity 清楚,明晰
- class action lawsuit 集體訴訟
- classified (advertisement) 分類的

- classified (document) 保密的
- clear - convincing evidence 清晰和令人信服的證據
- clear and present danger 迫在眉睫的危險
- clearing house 結算所,票據交換所
- clerk of the court 法庭書記
- close of pleading 答辯結束,诉讼辩论结束
- closing argument 終結陳述、終結辯論
- closing date 結帳日期
- closing entry 結帳分錄
- closing stock 期末存貨
- closing the books 結帳
- club accounts 社團會計,非牟利組織會計
- cocaine 古柯鹼、白粉
- co-conspirator 共謀人、篡謀人
- code of conduct 行為准則
- code of ethics 專業操守,道德守則,道德規約
- code of practice 工作守則,實務守則,執業守則
- codicil 遺囑修改附录,遗嘱修订附件,遗嘱附加书
- codification 編集成典,法律編纂
- coercion 強迫,压制,威逼

- coercive power 強制權力
- cognizance of the court 法院审理权
- cohabitation 同居,姘居
- coinsurance 共負保險
- collateral 抵押品
- collateral attack 並行的攻擊
- collateral review 並行覆核
- collect call 接聽人付費長途電話
- collective bargaining 集體議價,集體談判
- collective ownership 集體所有,集體所有制
- collusion 共谋,勾结,串通,串骗
- columnar account 多欄式帳戶
- columnar presentation 多欄式報導
- come clean 全盘招供,和盘托出
- come into force 生效
- command 命令,指令,指揮
- commerce 商業,商貿
- commercial balance sheet 商业资产平衡表
- commercial banks 银行
- commercial bribe receiving 收受商業賄賂

- commercial bribing    商業賄賂
- commercial code    商业法典
- commercial drivers license    商業性駕駛執照
- commercial law    商事法,商务法,商法
- commercial paper    商業票據
- commit a crime    犯下罪行
- commit murder    谋杀
- commitment    承諾
- commitment hearing    拘禁聽證
- committed cost    約束成本,已承擔成本
- committed for trial    拘押候审
- committed to prison    被判入狱
- committee structure    委員會結構
- commodities futures market    商品期貨市場
- commodity    商品
- commodity exchange    商品交易所
- common carrier    運輸業,承運商
- common    共用的,共有的,普通的,一般的
- common law    判例法、習慣法、普通法
- common law marriage    普通法/習慣法上的婚姻

- common property  共同财产,公有物
- common stock  普通股
- commotion  骚动,混乱
- communal  公共的,公有的,公社的
- communication  通信,通讯,交换,交流,交往
- communiqué  公报
- communism  共產主意
- community court  社區法院
- community service  社区服务
- community service  社區服務
- community standards  共同道德標準
- community tax  社区税
- commutation  減刑
- Companies Ordinance  公司條例
- Companies Registry  公司註冊處
- company  公司,商号,同伴,交往
- company accounts  公司會計
- company act  公司法案
- company law  公司法
- company limited by guarantee  擔保有限公司

- company officer with statutory    经理、代理人
- comparability    可比性
- comparative advantage    比較優勢
- comparative balance sheet    比較資產負債表
- comparative statement    比較報表
- compelling argument    有道理/有説服力的爭辯
- compensable    应予以补偿, 可补偿
- compensating balance    補償性最低存款額
- compensating error    抵銷性錯誤
- compensation    补偿, 赔偿
- compensation for damage    损失赔偿
- compensation management    報酬與福利管理
- compensation survey    報酬與福利調查
- compensatory balance    補償性最低存款額
- competence    能力、權限
- competence of defendant    被告的意識能力
- competency    资格, 权限, 作证能力
- competent    有权能的, 主管的, 能胜任的
- competent authorities    主管当局
- competent council    合格的律師

- competent court　管轄法院、主管法院
- competent evidence　有效的證據
- competent to stand trial　有受審能力
- competitive advantage　競爭優勢
- competitive advertising　競爭性廣告
- complain　投诉,申诉,控诉,控告
- complaint　投诉,控告,起诉
- completed transaction　完整會計事項
- completeness　完整
- completion　完成,实现
- compliance　履行,遵从,遵照,遵守
- component　組成元素,元件
- compound　和解,妥协
- compound interest　利滾利
- compounding　複息
- compulsory　强制的,强迫的
- compulsory education　義務教育
- compulsory liquidation　強制清盤
- compulsory process　強制到庭的程序
- computer crimes　用計算機（電腦）犯罪

- computer tampering 電腦篡改
- computer trespass 電腦侵入
- computerised accounting 電腦化會計
- concealed firearm 夾帶/夾藏的槍械
- concealed weapon 夾帶/夾藏武器、暗器
- concealment 隐蔽,隐藏,隐瞒
- concede 承认,接受,让与
- concept stock 概念股 , 概念股票
- conceptual skill 概念技能
- concerted 一致,共同,协调
- concession 特许,让与,租让
- conciliation 和解,調停,調解,斡旋
- conciliator 調停人,調解人
- conciseness 簡明
- conclusive 决定性推定
- conclusive judgement 最后判决
- concreteness 具體
- concurrent sentences 合併刑期、同時執行
- condemnation 谴责
- condemned prisoner 死囚,死刑犯

- condition    条件,条款,状况
- condition of validity    有效条件
- conditional discharge    有条件释放
- conditional legacy    附条件遗赠
- conditional promise    有条件的许诺
- conditional release/discharge    有條件釋放
- conditions of parole    假釋條件
- conditions of probation    守行為的條件
- conditions of release    釋放條件
- condonation    宽恕,不咎
- conduct    行为,处理,举动,品格,操行,进行
- confess one's guilt    供认有罪
- confess    供认
- confession    供认,招供,自白书
- confidence game    骗局
- confidence man    骗子
- confidence    信任,信赖,自信,信心
- confidential    机密的
- confidential communication    通讯秘密(的特权)
- confidential information    机密情报,机密资料

- confidentiality　保密性、機密性
- confine　禁閉,監禁,限制
- confinement　監禁,限制,拘留
- confirmed letter of credit　保兌信用狀
- confiscate　沒收、充公
- confiscation　没收,充公
- confiscated goods　没收的货物
- confiscation of property　没收财产
- conflict of interest　利益衝突
- conform　遵照,符合,一致
- confrontation of witness　證人對質
- conglomerate　聯合企業
- conjecture　推測,猜測
- conjugal rights　夫妻同居权
- conjugal　婚姻的,夫妇的
- connivance　默许,纵容
- conscription　征兵,征募
- consecutive　连续的,连接的,连贯的,依次的
- consensual　经双方同意的
- consensus ad idem　意见一致

- consent 准许,同意
- consequences 结果,后果,重要性,重要地位
- consequential damage 间接损失,后果的损失
- consequential loss 災後損失,後果性損失
- conservatism 穩健保守
- consideration 报酬,约因,酬劳,代价,补偿
- consigned goods 委托物,寄销品
- consignment note 托運通知書
- consignment stocks 委托代销货物、寄售货物
- consignment 委托,寄售
- consistency 一貫性,一致性 ，一貫原則
- consolidated balance sheet 綜合資產負債表
- consolidated financial statement 綜合財務報告表
- consolidated group 合併集團
- consolidated income statement 綜合損益表
- consolidated surplus 合併盈餘
- consolidated working fund 合併營運基金
- consolidation goodwill 合併商譽
- consolidation 合并,联合
- conspiracy to commit a crime 篡謀犯罪

- conspiracy 共謀、篡謀
- constable 警察
- constituent company 分子公司,成員公司
- constitutional law 宪法
- constitutional right 憲法權利
- constraint 拘束,拘禁,限制,強迫
- construction 法律释义,解释,建设
- construction in progress 在建工程
- construction of law 法律释义
- consular invoice 領事簽證單,領事發票
- consumer behaviour 消費者行為
- Consumer Council Ordinance 消費者委員會條例
- consumer credit 消費者信貸
- consumer goods 消费品,消费物资
- consumer loyalty 消費者忠誠
- consumer market 消費者市場 , 個人消費市場
- consumer preference 消費者偏好
- consumer price index 消費物價指數
- consumer responsibilities 消費者責任
- consumer rights 消費者權利

- consumer survey　消費者調查
- consumerism　消費者主義
- consummate　圓房,完婚,完善
- consumption strategy　消費策略
- consumption　消費
- container accounts　盛器會計,包裝物會計
- container　貨櫃,貨箱
- containerization　貨櫃運輸,貨櫃化
- contempt of court　蔑視法庭
- contempt　蔑視,藐視
- contention　爭论,论点
- contentious　引起爭论的,爭执的,诉讼的
- contestable　可爭论的
- contingency fund　意外準備基金,應急基金
- contingency　偶发事件,意外事故,未来事件
- contingent annuity　或有年金
- contingent asset　或有資產
- contingent charge　或有費用
- contingent liabilities　或有债务
- continuance (of the case)　訴訟延期、展延

- continuity postulate　持續經營假設
- continuous production　連續性生產,流水生產
- contra account　对销帐户,抵销帐户
- contra entry　對銷分錄,抵銷分錄
- contract authorization　訂約授權數
- contract　契约,合同,承包契约,缔结,订约,承包
- contract law　合同法、契約法
- contract of indemnity　赔偿契约,损失赔偿合同
- contract of marriage　婚约,婚姻契约
- contract of service　劳务合同,服务契约
- contract price　合約價格
- contradict　反駁
- contradiction　矛盾,反证,反驳
- contravention　违反,抵触,触犯
- contributed capital　实缴资本
- contribution chart　貢獻毛益圖
- contribution margin　獲利差額,毛利,邊際貢獻
- contribution to sales　貢獻毛益率
- contribution　貢獻毛益
- contributory　有助于,促成,负连带责任,起作用

- control account    統制帳戶
- control agreement, dependency 管理合同、监督协议
- control chart    控制圖
- control unit    控制部件
- controllable cost    可控制之成本
- controlled company    分公司,受制公司
- controlled junction    設有交通灯的交界路口
- Controlled substance    受管制藥物
- controller    會計長,主計長,綜計長,管制長
- controlling account    統制帳戶
- controlling company    總公司,控股公司
- controlling interest    控制權益,控制股權
- controlling shareholder    控股股東,具控制權股東
- convenience goods    便利品
- convenience store    便利店,便利店舖
- convention    慣例
- convertible bond    可調換公司債券,可換債券
- convertible loan stock    可轉換債券
- convertible preference share    可轉換優先股
- conveyance of property    財产转让

- convict 犯罪
- to convict 定罪
- convicted prisoner 被定罪的罪犯
- conviction quashed 推翻原判
- conviction 定罪、判罪
- convince 信服
- convincing 令人信服的,有说服力的
- cooling-off period 冷却期,冷静期,等待期
- co-operative society 合作社
- co-operative 生產人合作社
- co-ordinate system 座標制度
- co-ordination 協調
- co-partner 合夥人
- copyright 版权
- corovner 验尸官
- coroner's court 验尸庭
- corporal punishment 体罚,肉刑
- corporal 肉体的
- corporate 公司的,法人的,社团的,团体的
- corporate body 法人,法人团体/组织

- corporate governance statement　公司治理声明
- corporate governance　公司管治
- corporate property　公司财产，法人财产
- corporate social responsibility　企業社會責任
- corporation tax law　公司稅法、法人稅法
- corporation tax　公司稅
- corporation　公司,法團
- corporeal property　有形财产(土地或物品)
- correcting entry　更正分錄
- correction of error　錯誤更正
- corrections officer　懲教官，獄卒
- corrective training　改造训练
- corroborate　证实 證實
- corroboration　確實
- cost　成本
- cost accounting　成本會計
- cost allocation　成本分配
- cost analysis　成本分析
- cost centre　成本中心
- cost classification　成本分類

- cost concept　成本觀念
- cost control　成本控制
- cost distribution sheet　企业成本核算单
- cost of capital　資本成本,資金成本
- cost of completed goods　製成品成本
- cost of control　控制成本
- cost of goods manufactured　製成品成本
- cost of goods sold　銷貨成本,銷售成本
- cost of sales　銷貨成本
- cost-benefit analysis 成本收益分析,成本效益分析
- cost-effectiveness analysis　成本效能分析
- costing　成本会计
- cost-plus pricing 成本加成定價,成本加利潤計價法
- cost-plus　成本加成
- costs incurred　所引起的費用
- cost-volume-profit analysis　本量利分析法
- counsel　律師
- counseling　辅导,指导,商议
- count　罪項
- counter offer　还价

- counterfeit 伪造,假冒,冒牌
- counterfeiting 偽造
- counterfoil 存根,票根
- counterfoil receipt 存根收据
- countermand 取消,撤回,召回
- country of origin 原籍国,原产国,出产国
- coupon bond 息票債券
- coupon rate 票面利率
- courier service 速遞服務
- court 法庭、法院
- court appearance 出庭
- court appointed attorney 法庭任命的律師
- court clerk 法庭書記
- court decorum 法庭礼仪
- court interpreter 法庭翻譯、法庭傳譯
- court of appeals 上訴法院
- court of civil appeal 民事上诉庭
- court of criminal appeal 刑事上诉庭
- court of equity 衡平法庭
- court of first instance 初审法庭,第一审法庭

- court of inquiry 调查法庭,调查庭
- court of justice 法院,法庭
- court of last resort 終審法院
- court of record 案件紀錄所在的法院
- court order 法令
- court part 法庭
- cover 庇护,借口,负担支付,弥补,投保,隐匿
- cover note 临时保单,承保条
- cover up 掩饰
- coverage 赔偿债务的准备金总额
- covered warrant 備兌認股權證,回購認股證
- crack 快克
- craft union 同業工會
- credibility 可信程度,确实性,可靠性
- credible witness 可信的证人,可靠证人
- credible 可信的,可靠的
- credit 貸方,貸項,貸記,貸入
- credit analysis 信用分析
- credit balance 存款、贷方余额
- credit card 信用卡

- credit control　信用控制,信貸控制
- credit entry　贷方分录
- credit insurance　信用保險,信貸保險
- credit line　信用限額,信貸限額
- credit management　信用管理,信貸管理
- credit memorandum　貸項通知單
- credit note　貸項通知單,入帳通知書
- credit period　賒帳期間,信用期限
- credit policy　信用政策,信貸政策
- credit rating　信用評級,信貸評級
- credit sale　賒售,賒銷
- credit term　賒帳條件
- credit transfer　貸項轉帳
- credit union　儲蓄互助社,信用社
- creditor　债权人、债主
- creditors ledger　應付帳款分類帳,債權人分類帳
- crime　罪行
- crime lab　罪證化驗室
- crime of forgery　伪造罪
- crime of perjury　伪证罪

- crime of terrorism　恐怖主義罪
- crime of violence　暴力罪行
- crime scene　犯罪現場
- criminal　罪犯,犯罪的
- criminal background information　前科資料
- criminal case　刑事案件
- criminal code　刑事法典
- criminal conduct　犯罪行為
- criminal contempt　刑事上藐視法庭
- criminal court　刑事法庭
- criminal damage　刑事損失
- criminal element　犯罪因素/要素
- criminal facilitation　方便或便利他人犯罪
- criminal impersonation　假冒他人身份
- criminal informationn　刑事檢舉書
- criminal intent　犯罪意圖
- criminal jurisdiction　刑事审判权,刑事司法管辖权
- criminal justice　刑事司法
- criminal law　刑事法
- criminal libel　刑事诽谤

- criminal matter (s)　刑事事件,刑事案件
- criminal misappropriation　刑事盜用/挪用
- criminal mischief　刑事惡作劇
- criminal mischief　刑事的恶作剧行为
- criminal negligence　刑事疏忽
- criminal nuisance　刑事滋擾
- criminal offence　刑事罪,刑事罪行
- criminal penalty　刑事惩罚,刑罚
- criminal possession of a weapon　非法持有武器
- criminal possession　非法擁有
- criminal procedure　刑事诉讼程序
- criminal proceedings　刑事訴訟程序
- criminal prosecution　刑事检控
- Criminal purchase of a weapon　非法購買武器
- criminal record　犯罪記錄
- criminal responsibility　刑事责任
- criminal sale of a firearm　非法銷售軍火
- criminal sale of marijuana　非法銷售大麻
- criminal simulation　非法模似
- criminal solicitation　非法教唆

- criminal suit　刑事诉讼
- criminal tampering　非法干预
- criminal trespass　非法侵入他人土地或房屋罪
- criminal use of a firearm　非法使用軍火
- criminal usury　非法高利貸
- criminal violence　暴力罪行
- criminal wrong　刑事过失／犯罪
- criminally negligent homicide　刑事疏忽殺人
- criminate　告发,控告,归罪,陷人于罪,牵累
- cross complaints　相互控诉/指控,反诉
- crossed cheque　劃線支票
- crosswalk　行人穿越道、斑馬綫、人行道
- crowbar　铁撬
- crucial problem　决定性问题
- culpability　罪責
- culpable negligence　负有罪责的疏忽
- cum dividend　帶息
- cumulative dividend　累積股息
- cumulative frequency　累積頻率,累積頻數
- cumulative legacy　累积遗赠,附加遗赠

- cumulative preference share　累積優先股
- cumulative preferred stock　累積優先股
- cumulative sentence　累積刑期
- curfew　宵禁、戒嚴
- curia advisari vult　延期判決
- currency　貨幣,流通,流传,传播
- current account　往來存款帳戶,活期存款帳戶
- current assets　流动资产
- current cost accounting　現時成本會計
- current cost　現時成本
- current deposit　活期存款
- current expenditure　本期支出
- current fund　流動基金,流動資金
- current investment　短期投資
- current liability　流動負債,短期負債
- current money　通用的货币
- current price　現價,時價
- current purchasing power　現時購買力
- current ratio　流動比率
- current replacement cost　現時重置成本

- current replacement value　重置价值、替换值
- current return　本期報酬
- custodial interference　妨礙監護權
- custodial sentence　判处监禁
- custodian　保管人,监护人
- custody　保管,监护,监禁,拘留,拘押
- custody for trial　拘押候审
- custody of children　儿女抚养(权)
- custom duty　關稅
- customary marriage　风俗婚姻,传统婚姻
- customary　习俗的,惯有的,依习惯的
- customer　客户、用户
- customer behavior　顧客行為
- customer departmentalisation　顧客分部
- customer list　客户名单
- customers ledger　客戶分類帳
- cut-off　截止
- cut-off date　截止日期
- cut-off procedure　截結程序
- cut-off　截止

- cut-throat competition    惡性競爭，割頸式競爭
- cutting into the path    越侵车道
- cyclical fluctuation    週期性波動
- cyclical unemployment    週期性失業

# D

- damage 损害,损失,破坏,毁坏
- damnify 损伤,损害,伤害
- damning 异致定罪的,认定...有罪的
- damning evidence 有罪确证,有罪的证据
- damnum 损害,损失
- damnum absque injuria 不能依法给予补救的损害
- damnum injuria datum 非法损害他人财物
- dangerous driving 危险驾驶
- dangerous instrument 危險器具
- dangerous weapon 危险性武器
- data 數據、資料
- data bank 数据库
- data collection method 資料搜集方法
- data processing 數據處理
- data transmission 數據傳輸
- date of acquisition 購置日期,取得日期

- day of hearing 审讯日期,审讯日,审理日
- day of maturity 期满之日,到期之日
- days of grace 寬限日
- days' purchases in accounts payable 賒購期限
- days' sales in accounts receivable 賒銷期限
- de facto 事實上、實際上
- de facto director 实际董事
- de jure 法理上
- de novo 重新,重新审理
- de novo law 重订的法律
- deadly physical force 致命武力
- deadly weapon 致命武器
- death 死亡,剥夺政治权利,灭亡
- death by misadventure 意外致死
- death certificate 死亡证书
- death in line of duty 因公殉职
- death penalty 死刑
- death warrant 死刑执行令
- debate 辯論
- debenture 信用債券

- debenture capital 信用資本,信用債券式資本
- debit 借方,借項,借記,借入
- debit entry 借方分录[记帐]
- debit memorandum 借項通知單,支帳通知書
- debit note 借項通知單,支帳通知書
- debrief (a witness) 詢問（證人）
- debt 債,債務
- debt capital 債務資本,借入資本
- debt discount 債務折扣
- debt finance 外借資金
- debt financing 舉債,債務籌措,舉債融資
- debt management 債務管理
- debt of record 诉讼记录所证明的债务
- debt provable in bankruptcy 宣告破产时确认的债务
- debt ratio 債務比率
- debt-equity ratio 債務與資本比率
- debtor 债务人,负债者
- debtor summons 债务人传票
- debtors ledger 應收帳款分類帳,債務人分類帳
- decease 死亡

- deceit　欺骗,诈欺,虛伪
- decentralization　分散，分權,權力分散
- decentralised authority　分權,權力分散
- decentralised management　分權管理,分層管理
- deception　欺瞞、矇騙
- decision　判决,裁定,决议,决定
- declarant　述者,宣誓者,供述人,申报人,声明人
- declaration　供述,声明,宣誓,宣告,陈述,宣言
- declared dividend　已宣佈股利
- declared value　設定價值
- decline stage　衰退期
- decline to prosecute　拒絕起訴
- declining-balance method　餘額遞減折舊法
- decree　判决,判令,裁决,裁定,政令,命令
- decree nisi　中期判决,非绝对判决
- decree of nullity of marriage　宣告婚姻无效的判决
- decrement　貶值,減值
- deductible　可抵扣的
- deed　契据,契约,文据,证书,行为,事业
- deed of gift　赠与契据,赠与证书

- deed of indemnity　赔偿契据
- deed of separation　分居协议,分居证书
- deed of settlement　协议契据,财产授与契据
- deemed　认为,被视为
- deemed fit and proper　视为正当
- deface　毁损,毁伤外貌,破坏外观,销毁
- defalcation　盗用公款,监守自盗,亏空
- defamation　诽谤,中伤,破坏名誉
- defamatory libel　诽谤名誉
- defamatory matter　诽谤性事项
- default　不履行,违约,不到案,拖欠,玩忽,缺席
- default interest　滞延付款利息
- default judgment　缺席判决
- default of appearance　不出庭,不到案
- default of defence　无答辩
- defaulter　违约者,亏空公款者,不出庭者,犯军纪者
- defective　有缺点的,有缺陷的,有瑕疵的
- defence　辩护,答辩,辩方,被告,抗辩,防卸,防护
- defence of provocation　以挑衅为理由的辩护
- defence witness　被告证人,辩方证人

- defendant　被告,答辯人
- defense　辯護、答辯、辯方
- defense attorney　辯護律師
- defense counsel/lawyer　辯護律師
- defense exhibit　辯方呈物甲/證物甲
- deferment　延期
- deferral　延期
- deferred asset　遞延資產
- deferred charge　遞延借項,遞延費用
- deferred expenditure　遞延支出
- deferred liability　遞延負債
- deferred prosecution　緩期起訴
- deferred tax asset　递延所得税资产
- deferred taxes　递延税项
- deficiency　短交額,短欠,虧損,不足
- deficiency account　虧絀帳戶
- deficiency appropriation　補撥款
- deficit　虧絀,赤字,虧損
- defined benefit plan　界定福利计划
- defined contribution plan　界定供款计划

- definite sentence　有期徒刑
- defraud　詐騙、欺詐
- defunct　已死的、已故的、已倒閉的
- degree　轻重,等级,程度,学位
- degressiv declining　衰退的
- del credere　擔保還款
- del credere agent　包銷商,保付貨價代理人
- del credere commission　擔保還款佣金
- delegation of authority　授權
- deletion　删除
- deliberation　慎重考虑,商讨,审议,商议
- delinquency　少年犯罪,犯罪行为,过失,失职
- delinquent　少年犯
- delirium　精神错乱,神智不清
- delivered price　交貨價格
- delivery　供货
- demand　需求、询价
- demise　转让,遗赠,出租,让与,传,转移,死亡
- democratic leadership　民主式領導
- demolish　拆毀、拆除

- demolition 拆毁,废止,取消,破坏,毁损
- demonstrable 可论证的,可证明的,可表明的
- demonstrate 论证,证明,证实,表示,表明,示范
- demonstration 论证,证明,实证,确证,示威
- demotion 降,降級
- demur 抗辩,抗议,异议
- demurrable 可抗辩的
- demurrage 滯期費、逾期停泊費
- denounce 譴責、斥責、駁斥
- deny (a charge) 否認、否定
- deny (a request or proposal) 駁回、否決
- department of corrections 獄政局、監獄局、勞改局
- department of public safety 公安局、公安機關
- departmentalization 部門劃分,部門化,分部
- departmentation 部門劃分,部門化
- dependant parents 受贍养的父母
- depleted cost 耗餘成本
- deploy 調配,調派,部署
- deplume 剥夺(财产/荣誉等)
- deportation 遞解出境、驅逐出境

- deposit 存款,保證金,定金,押金
- deposit protection scheme 存款保險計畫
- deposition 宣誓證言、宣誓證詞
- depositor 存戶
- deposits paid 已付預付保证金款
- deposits received 已收預付保证金款
- deposit-taking company 接受存款公司
- deprave 腐化、腐敗
- depreciable amount 應折舊額
- depreciable asset 應折舊資產
- depreciation 折舊,貶值,損耗
- depreciation allowance 折舊金,折舊提存
- depreciation fund 折舊基金
- depreciation rate 折舊率
- depreciation reserve 折舊準備
- depreciation unit 折舊單位
- depression 不景气,萧条,沮丧,抑郁,消沉,凹陷
- depressive insanity 抑郁性精神病
- deputy sheriff 警員
- deregulation 放松管制

- derelict  遗弃物,无主物
- dereliction  遗弃,疏忽职守,放弃
- derivative  衍生工具
- derogatory  诽谤的,贬低的,毁损的
- desecration  亵渎、侮辱
- deserted children  被遗弃的子女
- deserted wife  被遗弃的妻子
- desertion  遗弃,擅离职守
- designate  指明,称呼,委任,指定
- designated felony act  指定重罪行为
- designation  选派,任命,称号,指定,选任
- desire  愿望,心愿,欲望,期望,希望
- destruction of property  破坏财务
- detain  扣留、拘留
- detainee  被拘留者
- detainer  扣押令
- detention  拘留,扣押,拘役,监禁
- detention order  拘押令,拘留令
- detention warrant  拘留令,拘押令
- detention without trial  未经审讯拘留

- determinate sentence   有期徒刑
- determination   决心,决定,终结
- deterrent   制止的,威慑的,制止因素,威慑因素
- detinue   请求返还扣留物的诉讼
- detoxification   戒毒
- detriment   损害,伤害,危害
- detrimental   有害的,不利的
- devaluation   贬值
- devalue   贬值,降低
- devastavit   怠忽管理遗产的责任,遗产毁损/浪费
- development   发展
- deviation, variance   偏差,变动
- device   设计,方法,手段,仪器,诡计,计策
- devilling   为律师代撰诉状,为作家代写文章
- devise   土地遗赠,不动产遗赠
- devisor   遗赠者,遗产赠与者
- devolution   (责任、权利等的)转移,授权代理
- devolution of authority   权力移交
- devolution of intestacy   无遗嘱的财产继承
- devolution of title   产权继承

- diagnosis 診斷
- dictum 法官意见,附带意见,名言,格言
- dies a quo 起算日
- differential cost 差量成本
- differential product 差異產品
- differentiated marketing 差異營銷
- differentiation 分化,区别化
- diminution 贬值
- direct compensation 直接報酬
- direct cost 直接成本
- direct costing 直接成本法
- direct credit 直接貸記
- direct damage 直接损失,直接损害
- direct debit 直接支帳付款,直接扣帳
- direct distribution 直接分銷,直接分配
- direct evidence 直接證據
- direct examination 直接詢問
- direct expense 直接成本,直接費用
- direct labour 直接人工
- direct mail 推銷郵件

- direct marketing　直接行銷
- direct material　直接原料
- direct shipment　直接裝運
- direct write-off method　直接銷帳法
- directed verdict　指令裁決
- directing　指揮
- director　公司董事,理事,主任
- director's emolument　董事津貼
- director's remuneration　董事酬金
- director's report　董事報告
- directors' fee　董事报酬
- disability insurance　傷殘保險
- disability　无行为能力,无资格,伤残
- disallow　拒绝接受,拒绝承认,不允许,不批准
- disapproval　不批准,不赞成
- disavowal　拒絕承擔責任
- disbar　取消律师资格,将某律师除名
- disburse　支付
- disbursement　支付款项
- discharge of debt　消偿债务

- discharge　解除,释放,解雇,解职,免除履行
- disciplinary action　紀律處分
- disciplinary offence　违反纪律罪
- discipline　纪律,风纪,惩戒,惩罚
- disclosure requirement　表露要求, 披露要求
- discount　折扣，貼現，折價
- discount allowed　銷貨折扣
- discount house　貼現公司,票據貼現所,貼現行
- discount of bill　汇票贴现
- discount on debenture　債券折價
- discount on share　股票折價
- discount received　購貨折扣
- discounted cash flow　折現現金流量
- discounting bill of exchange　票據貼現
- discovery　告知準備使用的證據、透露證據
- discredit　丧失信用,不相信,不信任,诋毁
- discrepancy　不一致,不符
- discretion　斟酌决定/处理(权),酌情处理,辨别
- discretionary income　自由支配收入,自由支配所得
- discrimination　不公平待遇,歧视,区别,辨别

- discriminatory pricing　歧視性定價
- discussion　讨论,谈论
- disease　疾病
- dishonor　拒付,拒絕付款,拒絕承兌
- dishonoured cheque　退票,不兌現支票,拒付支票
- dismantling cost　弃置成本
- dismemberment　肢解
- dismiss　駁回
- dismiss a case　撤銷案件
- dismiss with prejudice　有偏見駁回起訴
- dismiss without prejudice　無偏見駁回起訴
- dismissal 驳回,免职,遣散,不予处理,撤销(诉讼)
- disorderly conduct　騷擾公眾秩序
- disparity　不一致,不等,差异
- disparity of sentence　刑罰差距,判決差別
- dispensation 特免,豁免,分配,处置,处理,执行
- disposable income　可用所得,可支配收益
- disposal of asset　資產處理,資產變賣
- disposal　处理,处置,安排,布置
- disposition　處理

- dispositional hearing　處置聆訊
- dispossession　夺取,剥夺,强占,驱逐
- dispute　争执,纠纷,争论,争辩
- disqualification　取消资格,无资格,不合格
- dissension　异议,意见分歧,纷争,冲突
- dissident　异議人士、持不同政見者
- dissolution　解约,解除,解散,终止,瓦解
- dissolution of contract　解约
- distraint　扣押财物,扣押
- distress　扣押,扣押财物,痛苦,遇难,苦恼
- distress warrant　财产扣押令
- distribution　(财产)分配,配给,分销
- distribution expense　推銷費用,分銷費用
- distribution restriction　分红限制
- distribution　分红
- distributor　經銷商,分銷商
- district Attorney (DA)　地方檢察官 (DA)
- disturbance　極端激動的情緒
- disturbing public meeting　擾亂公眾會議
- disturbing the peace　擾亂治安

- diversification   多元化,多樣化,分散
- diversion   轉移、替換
- divest   剝奪
- divestment   出盤,放棄,減少投資
- dividend   股息、股利
- dividend cover   股息比率，盈利對股息比率
- dividend policy   股息政策
- dividend yield   股息率
- division of labour   分工
- division of work   分工
- divorce petition   离婚申请书
- divorce proceedings   离婚诉讼
- divorce   离婚
- doctrine   学说,原则,主义,教务
- document   單據，文件
- document against acceptance   承兌交單
- document against payment   付款交單
- document of search   搜查证
- document of title   業權,所有權
- documentary   公文的,文件的,文据的,证书的

- documentary bill　跟單匯票
- documentary credit　跟單信用證
- documentary evidence　书面证据,文件证据
- doli incapax　无犯罪能力的,无犯意的,不应负责的
- domestic trade　本土貿易,國內貿易
- domestic violence　家庭暴力
- domicile　住所
- domicile, registered office　(公司)地址、所在地
- donatio ante nuptias　婚前赠与
- donatio inter vivos　生前赠与
- donatio mortis causa　临终前赠与
- donation　捐赠,捐款
- donee　受赠人
- donor　捐赠人,遗赠人,授权人
- dormant partner　不參與管理合夥人,匿名合夥人
- double column system　雙欄制
- double entry bookkeeping　复式簿记
- double taxation agreement　避免双重征税协定
- doubt　怀疑,疑惧,疑问,疑惑
- doubtful debt　壞帳,呆帳

- down payment　首期付款
- draft　匯票,草案,法案,草稿,图样,付款通知单
- draftsman　草拟人,议案起草人,法案起草人,起草人
- dragnet　法網
- drive-by shooting　駛過槍擊
- driver's education　駕駛培訓
- driving licence　驾驶执照
- driving on a suspended license　车在駕照吊銷期間開車
- driving record　駕駛紀錄
- driving　驾驶,力量,精力,能力
- drug　药品,毒品
- drug abuse　濫用毒品
- drug addict　癮君子
- drug addiction　毒癮
- drug bust　突擊搜捕毒品及販毒者
- drug counseling　戒毒輔導
- drug courier/mule　運毒者
- drug dealer　販毒者
- drug dependence　染有毒癮
- drug paraphernalia　服毒器具

- drug rehabilitation center　戒毒中心
- drug testing　藥物測試
- drug trafficking　販毒
- drunk driving　酒後開車
- drunkenness　醉酒，酩酊
- dual aspect concept　複式觀念
- duality　複式
- due care　应有的谨慎,应有的小心
- due consideration　适当的考虑
- due date　到期日
- due process of the law　適當/應有的法律程序
- due process　正当程序/手续,法定诉讼程序
- due　正当的,应得的,应付给的,期满
- due-diligence　盡職查證,盡責調查,仔細審查
- duly sworn　正式發誓
- dumping　傾銷
- duplicate　副本,复制品
- durable goods　耐用物品
- duress　威嚇，強迫
- duty　稅，職務,責任

- duty drawback 退稅
- duty list 職責表
- duty of care 对他人的安全应有的谨慎,抚养责任
- duty roster 輪值表
- dying declaration 临终遗言,临终声明

# E

- earning capacity 收益能力,盈利能力
- earning-capacity value 收益能力值
- earnings 收益,盈利
- easement 地役权
- eavesdropping 竊聽、偷聽
- economic co-operation 經濟合作
- economic cycle 经济状况
- economies of scale 規模經濟
- ecstasy 狂喜,搖頭丸
- education levy 教育費附加
- effective communication 有效的溝通
- effective management 有效管理方法
- effective rate of return 實際回報率
- eject 逐出,驱逐,排斥
- ejectment 驱逐,赶走,收回土地或房屋的诉讼
- ejusdem generis 同类的,同样性质的

- electorate 选民,选区
- electronic banking 電子銀行服務
- electronic computer 電子計算機
- electronic filing system 电子入禀系统
- electronic monitoring 電子監視
- electronic road pricing 电子公路收费
- eligibility 有资格,合格
- eligibility check 资格检查
- elimination 抵銷
- embargo 禁止(通商),禁止(船只出入港口)
- embarrassment 窘迫,使负责
- embedded derivatives 嵌入衍生工具
- embezzle 盗用,监守自盗,侵吞
- embezzlement 盗用公款
- embrace 笼络,收买,拥抱,信奉
- emergency 紧急情况,非常时刻
- emergency certificate 紧急证书
- emergency fund 應急基金
- emergency medical service 急救服務
- emolument 薪酬,酬金,津贴

- emotional appeal　情感訴求
- empanel　选任,登记入,列入
- employee　雇员
- employee association　職工聯會
- employee benefits　职工薪酬
- employee counselling　員工輔導
- employee-oriented　員工導向,員工取向
- employer　雇主
- employment agency　職業介紹所
- employment　就业
- employment-related legislations　勞工有關法例
- empower　賦予權利
- encroachment　侵犯,侵占,蚕食,侵害
- encumbrance　保留數,財產留置權
- end of period (date)　截止日期
- end user　最終使用者
- endorse　在(支票等)背面签名,背书,签署,认可
- endorsed writ　背书令状
- endorsement　背書,批註,加簽
- endorsement in blank　无记名式背书

- endorsement in full 记名背书,全名背书
- endowment 捐赠,捐款,天赋,资金,基金
- endowment fund 留本基金
- endowment insurance 储蓄保险
- enforce 实施,(强制)执行,强制,强调
- enforceable 可实施的,强制执行的
- enforcement 实施,执行,强制执行
- enforcement of right 行使权利
- enhanced penalties 加重刑罰
- enlistment act 应募入伍法令
- enquiry, inquiry 询价、询问
- enterprise 企業
- entertain a motion 考慮動議
- entertainment expenses 业务招待费,交际费
- entitlement 權益
- entity concept 個體觀念
- entrepot 轉口港
- entrepreneur 企業家
- entrepreneurial spirit 企業家精神
- entrepreneurship 企業家精神

- entry (in register)　登记、记录
- entry of judgment　判決的登錄
- equal protection of laws　法律平等保護
- equal protection　平等保護/保障
- equalisation reserve　平衡準備
- equality　平等,同等,相等
- equitable distribution　公平分配
- equitable lien　衡平法留置权
- equitable right　衡平法上的权利
- equity　產權,主權,權益,股本,股權,股票
- equity capital　主權資本,權益資本,股本
- equity finance　主權資金
- equity financing　股票融資, 資本籌措, 權益籌資
- equity method　权益法
- error of commission　帳名調亂錯誤
- error of omission　遺漏錯誤
- error of original entry　原始分錄錯誤
- error of principle　原則性錯誤
- escape　逃走
- to escape　逃跑

- esprit de corps　團體精神
- estate duty　遗产税
- estate　财产,房地产,产业,遗产,继承的财产/遗产
- estimate　估计、估算
- estimation　预算,估价,估计,估定,评价,测定
- ethical issue　道德問題
- eviction　逐出,收回
- evidence　證據
- evidences of title　所有权证据
- ex parte proceedings　一造诉讼
- ex parte summons　单方面的传票,一方当事人传票
- ex parte　单方面的
- ex　除,在外
- examination　審查、發問、盤問
- examination of witness　盘问证人,讯问证人
- examination-in-chief　直接讯问
- exceptional item　例外項目
- excessive damages　超额赔偿金
- excessive force　過分的武力
- excessive sentence　过重的刑罚

- exchange  兌換，交換
- exchange control  外匯管制
- exchange fund  外匯基金
- exchange gain  汇兑收益
- exchange loss  汇兑损失
- exchange rate  汇率、外汇比价
- exchange rate, stock price  外汇比率,股票牌价
- exchange risk  汇率风险
- exclusionary rule  排除不合法證據的法規
- exclusive distribution  獨家經銷
- exclusive possession  独占,专有
- exclusive right  独／专有权
- exculpatory evidence  昭雪的证据
- excusable homicide  可原諒的殺人
- excuse  借口,辩解,理由,托辞,原谅,宽恕
- ex-dividend  除息(股價)
- execution debtor  债务执行人
- executive  行政,行政人員,執行人員
- exemption from  豁免
- exemption  豁免

- exercisable 可行使的
- ex-godown 倉庫交貨價,出倉價
- ex-gratia compensation 恩恤补偿
- ex-gratia payment 恩恤付款/款項
- ex-gratia 恩恤,作为优惠,出自恩惠
- exhibit 呈物、證物
- exoneration of bail 免除保釋金
- exoneration 證明無罪、免除責任
- expectancy damages 预期赔偿金
- expectation of life 估计寿命,预期寿命,平均寿命
- expected value 期望值
- expedited order 急速个人保护令
- expenditure budget 支出預算
- expenditure 支出
- expense 费用
- expense account 費用帳戶
- expense of performance 清偿费用,偿债费用
- expert evidence 专家证据,鉴定人证据
- expert power 權威權力
- expert witness 专家证人,鉴定人

- expert　专家,鉴定人,行家
- expertise　專才，專門知識,專家經驗
- expiration, expiry　有效期限，到期日
- expired cost　已過成本,已耗成本
- expiry date　期滿之日,失效之日,期滿日,失效日
- exploitation　利用、剝削
- explosive　炸藥、爆炸物
- export　出口
- export licence　出口許可證
- export trade　出口业务
- exporter　出口商
- export-oriented　出口主導,出口導向
- exposure draft　公開評論之初稿
- exposure　暴露
- express condition　明示条件
- express provision　明文規定
- expunge　刪除、剔除
- ex-rights　除權
- extension of time　延期
- external audit　獨立審計

- external financing 向外籌措資金,向外融資
- extort confession 迫供,逼供
- extortion 勒索
- extra dividend 額外股利,額外股息
- extractive industry 採掘工業
- extradite 引渡(逃犯)
- extrajudicial 在司法程序或范围外,法院以外的
- extraneous 外来的,范围外的
- extraordinary expenses 非经常费用
- extraordinary income 非常收益
- extraordinary item 非常項目
- extraordinary loss 非常損失
- extraordinary profit 非常利潤
- extraordinary result 非正常纯损益
- extrinsic reward 外在報酬
- ex-warehouse 倉庫交貨價,出倉價
- ex-works 出廠價,工廠交貨價
- eye witness 见证人,目击证人

# F

- fabricate evidence　偽造證據
- fabrication　捏造、偽造
- face value　票面值,面值
- facilitator　协调员
- facsimile　传真,电传真
- facsimile copy　传真本
- fact　事实,实情,真情,实际
- fact-finding hearing　事實調查聽證會
- factor　應收帳款數購商,經紀商,代理人
- factor analysis　因素分析
- factor of production　生產要素
- factory cost　製造成本
- factory expense　製造費用
- factory overhead　間接製造成本
- factum　(本人的)实际行为,事实陈述书,事实
- failure to appear　不出庭罪

- fair competition 公平競爭
- fair market value 公允市场价值
- fair trade 公平交易
- fair use 公平使用
- fair value 公允价值
- fallacy 謬論
- false 假的,虚伪的,伪造的
- false accusation 誣告罪
- false arrest 非法逮捕
- false declaration 虚报
- false imprisonment 非法拘禁
- false testimony 伪证,假证
- falsely reporting an incident 報假案
- falsification 弄虚作假,伪造,窜改,篡改
- falsification of account 造假帐,伪造账目
- falsification of documents 僞造文件
- falsification of evidence 僞造證據
- falsify 窜改,伪造,说谎
- falsify a record 窜改记录
- family Court 家庭法院

- family property 家产
- family violence 家庭暴力
- fatal 致命的,毁灭性的
- fatal blow 致命的打击
- fatal wound 致命伤
- fee 报酬
- felony 刑事重罪
- fencing 買賣贓物
- fiduciary 受托的,受信托的,信托的
- fiduciary capacity 受托人资格
- fiduciary guardian 受托监护人
- fiduciary relation 受托
- field sobriety test 現場清醒測驗
- fight 搏斗,打架,斗争
- file 卷宗
- to file 提交、提出（訴訟）
- file a motion 提交動議&
- file notice of appeal 提交上訴通知
- film censorship 电影检查,电影审查
- filtering 過濾

- final accounts　決算表,決算帳戶,期末帳目
- final call　最後催繳款
- final dividend　末期股息,末期股利
- final order　最后命令,最终命令
- final process　最后程序,最后诉讼阶段
- finance company　財務公司
- finance lease　融资租赁
- finance product　個人財務產品
- financial accounting　財務會計
- financial analysis　財務分析
- financial assets　金融资产
- financial control　財務管理,財務控制
- financial decision　財務決定
- financial incentive　財務獎勵
- financial institution　財務機構,金融機構
- financial instrument　金融工具
- financial intermediary　金融仲介機構
- financial leverage　財務挺率,槓率
- financial management　財務管理
- financial market　金融市場,財務市場

- financial performance  財務表現
- financial plan  理財計畫
- financial portfolio  金融投資組合
- financial position  財務狀況
- financial product  金融產品
- financial ratio  財務比率
- financial reporting  財務申報
- financial result  財务业绩
- financial service  金融服務
- financial situation  財務狀況
- financial statement  財務報表
- financial support  財務上的支援
- financial year  会计年度
- financing  融资
- find  拾得物、掘獲物
- to find  判定
- find a verdict  作出裁決,作出判決
- find somebody guilty  裁決某人有罪
- finding  判決、調查結果
- fine  罚款,罚金

- fingerprints 指紋
- finished goods 产成品
- finished stock 製成品
- fire code 防火規章
- fire insurance 火險
- fire loss 火災損失
- fire marshal 消防局長
- fire prevention 防火措施
- firearms 槍械
- firecrackers 鞭炮、爆竹
- fireworks 煙火、焰火、煙花
- firm 商號,商行,企業
- first degree murder 一級謀殺
- first hearing 第一審
- first offender 初犯者
- First-in first-out 先进先出
- first-line manager 第一線管理人員
- first-time adoption 首次执行
- first-time consolidation 首次合并
- fiscal period 會計期間,財政期間

- fiscal unity concept 合并纳税申报制度
- fiscal year 財政年度,會計年度
- fixed asset 固定資產
- fixed budget 固定預算
- fixed capital 固定資本
- fixed cost 固定成本
- fixed deposit 定期存款
- fixed instalment method 定額分期付款法
- fixed interest-bearing 定息的
- fixed liability 固定負債
- fixed overhead 固定間接製造成本
- fixed sentence 有期徒刑
- fixtures and fittings 裝修與裝置
- flagellate 鞭打
- flat organization 平扁組織
- flexible budget 彈性預算
- flextime 彈性工作時間
- floating asset 浮動資產
- floating capital 流動資本
- floating charge 流動抵押品

- floating currency　浮动货币
- floating debenture　浮動抵押公司債券
- flow chart　流程圖
- folio reference　參考帳頁
- force　武力
- to force　（法律、条约、规章等的）约束力,效力,武力
- forcible eviction　強制收回租地/财产
- forcible rape　強姦
- forcible touching　強行撫摸
- forecast　預測
- foreclosure order　取消赎回权令
- foreclosure　贖回權的取消
- foregone conclusion　未经商议即已决定的结论
- foreign corporation　外國公司
- foreign currency　外币
- foreign exchange　外匯
- foreign exchange control　外匯管制
- foreign exchange market　外匯市場
- foreign exchange rate　外幣匯率
- foreign exchange spot rate　即期汇率

- foreign trade    對外貿易
- foreigner    外国人
- foreman    工頭
- forensic expert    科学鉴定专家 法醫、科學鑑定專家
- forensic psychiatry    司法精神病學
- forensic science    科學鑑定學
- forfeit    放棄、失去
- forfeiture proceedings    没收程序
- forfeiture    喪失,没收,没收物,罰金
- forgery    伪造,伪造(罪),伪造(品),赝品
- forgery of document    伪造文件
- form utility    形式效用
- formal    正式的,正规的,形式上的,合乎格式的
- formal agreement    正式协议
- formal contract    正式合同 / 契约
- formal organization    正式組織
- formalities of law    法律手续
- formality    拘泥形式,拘谨,礼节,格式,规格
- formation expense    開辦費用
- fornication    私通

- forward contracts    远期合约
- forward integration    前向合併
- forward-looking    向前看的
- foster care    寄養
- foster home    寄養家庭、收養所
- foul language    粗話
- found liable    判定有責任
- founders' share    發起人股本
- four-eyes principle    四眼原則
- frame up    造假陷害
- franchise    專營權,特許權
- franchisor    特許權擁有人
- fraud    行騙、欺詐
- fraud, swindle    欺骗、欺诈
- fraudulent    诈欺的,欺骗性
- fraudulent intention    欺诈意图
- free currency    自由貨幣
- free enterprise    自由企業
- free port    自由港
- free price    自由價格

- free trade　自由貿易
- freedom from bias　全無偏差
- freedom of the press　新闻自由,出版自由
- freehold　永久業權,不動產所有權
- freehold land　永久土地,永遠保有的地產
- freehold property　有永久地权的房地产
- free-rein leadership　自由放任式領導
- free-trade zone　保税区,自由贸易区
- freight　運費
- freight inward　購貨運費
- freight outward　銷貨運費
- fringe benefit　額外利益,附帶福利,邊緣福利
- frisk　搜身
- full coverage　全保
- full disclosure　全面披露
- full liability　全部責任,全部負債
- functional authority　職權,功能性職權,職能權力
- functional discount　功能折扣
- functional organization　功能組織,職能組織
- fund flow　資金流轉

- fund manager　基金經理
- fundamental accounting concept　基本會計概念
- funds statement　資金表
- future value　未來值
- futures contract　期貨合約
- futures deal　期貨交易
- futures market　期貨市場
- futures price　期貨價格
- futures trading　期貨交易

# G

- gag order    禁止談論令
- gain    盈餘,利得
- gallows    絞刑台
- gambling    赌博,打赌,投机,冒险
- gaming    賭博、堵塞
- gang assault    群毆
- gang fight    纠党打斗
- gang rape    轮奸
- garnish    通知扣押(债务人的财产)
- gearing    資本借貸作用,資本槓桿作用 ，槓桿比率
- general administrative expenses    管理费用
- general allowance    普通准备金
- general average    共同海損
- general damages    一般损害赔偿
- general expense    雜費
- general fund    普通基金

- general ledger 总分类帐
- general manager 总经理
- general overhead 普通間接費用
- general partner 普通合夥人
- general partnership 普通合夥
- general provisions 总则,通则
- general reserve 普通盈餘準備
- genocide 種族滅絕
- gesturing violently 猛烈的打手势
- gift in trust 托管某人的捐赠
- gift inter vivos 生前赠与
- gift 赠品,赠与,捐赠,礼物,天赋
- gist （訴訟中的）主旨、要點、大意
- globalization 全球化
- goal oriented 目標指向
- going concern 繼續經營
- goods 货物,商品,物品,财物
- good behavior 品行良好
- good cause 正当理由
- good faith effort 有誠意的努力

- goods in progress　在產品,在製品
- goods in transit　在運品
- goods on consignment　寄銷品
- goods　貨物,商品,物品,財物
- goods, merchandise　商品
- goodwill　商譽
- government budget　政府財政預算
- grace period　寬限期
- grading　等級
- graffiti　塗鴉
- to graffiti　塗鴉
- graft　受賄、瀆職
- grand jury　大陪審團
- grand theft　重偷竊罪
- grant of probate　遗嘱验证,授予遗嘱的认证
- grass-roots　基层
- gratuitous　免费的,不收酬劳的,无偿的
- gravity of offence　罪行的严重性,严重罪行
- gravity　严重(性)
- graze　擦伤,擦过,掠过

- grievance 不滿、冤情
- grievous wounding 严重伤害
- grievously sinful 罪孽深重
- gross 总的,显著的,整个的,全部的,严重的
- gross book value 帳面總值,總帳面值
- gross loss 毛损
- gross margin 毛利
- gross misdemeanor 严重的不端行为,严重行为失检
- gross negligence 严重疏忽,严重过失
- gross profit / loss 销售毛损益
- gross profit ratio 毛利率
- gross profit 毛利
- gross revenue 總收入,總收益
- gross salary 工资总额
- gross sales 銷貨總額
- gross weight 毛重
- ground 理理由
- grounds of decision 判决理由,作出决定的理由
- group accounts 綜合會計,集團帳目
- group auditor 集团审计师

- group incentive plan　團體獎勵計畫
- growth stage　成長期,發展期
- guarantee　担保、保证
- guarantor　担保人、担保方
- guardian ad litem　訴訟監護人
- guardian　监护人,保护人,守护人
- guideline　指导
- guilt　有罪,罪,罪行,犯罪,内疚
- guiltless　无罪的,无辜的
- guilty　有罪的,犯罪的,自觉有罪的,内疚的
- guilty intention　犯罪意图,犯意
- guilty plea　認罪的答辯
- guilty verdict　有罪裁决
- gunshot wound　槍傷

# H

- habeas corpus  人身保护令,人身保护令状
- habitual  习惯(性)的,惯常的
- habitual criminal  惯犯,累犯
- habitual drunkard  经常酗酒者,酒徒,酒癖
- habitual offender  惯犯 惯犯
- habitual sex offender  性慣犯
- habitual violent offender  暴力慣犯
- hacker  黑客
- hallucinogen  幻覺劑
- handcuff  手銬
- handgun  手槍
- hanging matter  要处绞刑的案子,绞刑案件
- harassment  騷擾
- harbor a criminal  窝藏罪犯
- hard currency  硬币,硬通货
- harm  损害,伤害,危害

- hate crime　仇恨罪
- hazardous material　危害物品、危險材料
- hazing　戲弄、惡作劇
- head office　總店
- hearing　审讯,审理,听审,聆讯
- hearing adjourned　延期审讯,押后审讯
- hearing examiner　聽證官
- hearing time　审讯日期
- hearsay　傳聞
- hedge　套期保值
- hedge accounting　套期会计
- hedging　套期,套戥,對沖
- heroin　海洛因
- heterogeneity　異質性
- heterogeneous product　異質產品
- hidden reserve　秘密储备
- high　高的,高度的,高级的,高等的
- high court　高等法院
- high geared　高資本借貸比率
- high-handed　高压的,专横的

- highway   公路
- highway patrol   高速公路巡警
- hijacking   劫持
- hindering prosecution   妨礙檢舉
- hire purchase account   租購帳
- hire purchase agreement   租購合約
- hire purchase   分期付款购买
- hit and run   駕車肇事后逃跑
- hoax   騙局
- holding(s)   占有物,所有物,拥有,具有,租借地
- holding company   控股公司
- holding gain or loss   持有損益
- holding office   任职
- holding out   冒称,冒充,自称
- holding period   持有期間
- home detention   軟禁
- home trade   本土貿易,國內貿易
- homicide   杀人罪,杀人行为
- homogeneous product   同質產品
- horizontal integration   橫向合併,橫面結合

- horizontal merger    橫向合併
- hostage    人質
- hostile witness    有敵意的证人,恶意证人
- hostile witness    敵對證人
- hot pursuit    緊追
- hourly rate    計時工資
- housebreaking    入屋行窃
- human relations    人際關係
- human resources management    人力資源管理
- human resources planning    人力資源規畫
- human resources    人力資源
- human skill    人際關係技能
- hung jury    不能做出一致決斷的陪審團
- hunting certificate/license/permit    狩獵許可
- hunting tag    狩獵標牌
- hyperinflationary economies    恶性通货膨胀经济
- hypermarket    特級市場,大型超級市場

# I

- identification 身份証
- identity theft 身份盜竊
- idle capacity 閒置生產能力
- idle equipment 閒置設備
- ignorance 无知,愚昧,不知情
- ignorant error 出于无知的错误
- ignorant 无知的,愚昧的,不知情的
- ignorantia facti excusat 不知情者可以宽恕
- illegal 不合法的,非法的,违规的,违例的,违法的
- illegal act 非法行为,违法行为,不法行为
- illegal alien 非法拘留者
- illegal contract 违法合同/契约,非法合同/契约
- illegal detention 非法拘留
- illegal drug traffic 非法的毒品买卖,非法贩毒
- illegal encroachment 违法侵占,非法侵入
- illegal immigration 非法移民

- illegal imprisonment 非法监禁
- illegal interest 不法收益,非法权益
- illegal measures 不法措施
- illegal payment 非法付款,不当给付
- illegal possession of a gun 非法持有槍支
- illegal practice 非法／不法行为
- illegal restraint 非法限制
- illegal search and seizure 非法搜查和扣留
- illegal touting 非法兜售物品,非法招徕
- illegality 违法,不合法,非法,非法行为
- illegitimacy 非法(性),违法(性),私生,非婚生
- illegitimate 非法的, 私生的
- illegitimate children 私生子女,非婚生子女
- illegitimate intercourse 私通,通奸
- illegitimate sale 私卖
- illicit 非法
- illusory 錯覺的
- immediate cause 近因,直接原因
- immigration 移民,移居
- immigration hold 移民局扣留

- immigration law　移民法
- imminent　急迫的,逼在眉睫的
- imminent danger　眼前的危险,迫在眉睫的危险
- imminent peril　眼前的危险
- immoral　不道德的,猥亵的,淫荡的,道德败坏的
- immoral conduct　不道德的行为
- immoral contract　不道德的合同/契约
- immorality　不道德的行为,淫荡行为
- immovable property　不动产
- immunity　豁免權
- immunity from liability　責任豁免權
- immunity from prosecution　檢控豁免權
- impairment　减損,减值
- impairment loss　虧損
- impartial　不偏袒的,公正无私的,公平的
- impartiality　公正无私,公平,公正
- impasse　死胡同,绝境,僵局,死路
- impeach　控告,检举,弹劾,非难,责问
- impeachable　可控告的,可弹劾的,可怀疑的
- impeachment　弹劾,责问,控告,检举

- impeachment of witness 指責證人
- impediment 妨碍,障碍,法定婚姻的障碍,身体缺陷
- impersonal accounts 非人名帳戶
- impersonation 假冒,冒名頂替,模拟
- impersonation of judge 假扮法官
- impersonation of police officer 假扮警察
- implement 履行,执行,实施,生效,用具,工具
- implementation 实施
- implicate 牽連
- implied condition 默示条件,默认条件
- implied consent 默認、默示同意
- implied term 默示條款
- import 进口
- import duty 入口稅
- import licence 入口許可證
- import restriction 入口限制,進口限制
- importer 入口商
- impostor 冒名頂替者,江湖骗子
- impracticable 不能实际的,不能实行的,不切实际的
- imprest cash 定額周轉金,定額零用金,定額備用金

- imprest fund　定額資金
- imprest system　定額制度
- imprisonment　徒刑、下獄、坐牢、禁錮
- impropriety　不正当(的行为)
- improvement　改进
- impulse buying　衝動性購買,即興購買
- imputation　归罪,转嫁罪责,诋毁,非难,污名
- in camera　不公開
- in integrum restitutio 回复原状
- in session　開庭
- inadmissible　不能接纳的,不能承认的,不能允许
- inadmissible evidence　不能接受/不可采纳的证据
- incapacitated person　無自保能力人仕
- incapacity　无资格,无能力
- incarcerate　监禁,禁闭,入狱
- incarceration　監禁
- incendiary　纵火的,煽动的,放火的
- incentive pay　獎金
- incentive plan　刺激計畫,獎勵計畫
- incentive　誘因,獎勵,刺激,鼓勵

- incest 亂倫
- incestuous 乱伦的, 犯乱伦罪的
- inchoate offenses 犯罪未遂
- incidental damages 附带/附属的赔偿
- incite 煽動、鼓動
- incitement 煽动, 煽惑他人犯罪
- inciting to riot 煽动暴动, 煽动叛乱罪
- income 收益, 收入
- income account 收益帳戶
- income and expenditure account 收益與費用帳
- income and expense 收益及費用
- income in advance 預收收益
- income statement 收益表, 損益表
- income tax law 所得稅法
- income tax refund 所得稅退還
- income tax 所得稅, 入息稅
- incoming partner 新加入合夥人
- incommunicado 不得与外界接触的,
- incomplete record 不完整會計記錄
- inconsiderate 不替別人着想的

- inconsistency 不一致,前后矛盾
- incorporated company 注冊成為公司,法人公司
- incorporation 註冊,登記
- increment 增值
- incremental cost 增量成本
- incremental loss 增量損失
- incremental profit 增量利潤
- incriminate 歸罪、使負罪
- incriminating evidence 牵连(某人)的证据
- inculpate 连累(某人),归罪于,牵累
- inculpatory statement 可入罪供詞
- indebtedness 債務
- indecency 猥褻,下流言行,粗鄙
- indecent behavior 有伤风化
- indecent conduct 猥褻行為,下流行為,粗野的
- indecent exposure 不文暴露
- indemnity of loss 损失赔偿,损失补偿
- indemnity 赔偿,赔款,补偿,免罚,赦免,保障
- indent 國外訂貨單
- indenture 合約,契約

- indeterminate sentence 不定期徒刑
- index number 指數
- indication on costs 讼费指示
- indictment 大陪審團起訴述、大陪審團公訴述
- indigent 貧窮的
- indirect compensation 間接報酬
- indirect cost 間接成本
- indirect evidence 間接證據
- indirect expense 間接費用
- indirect labour 間接人工
- indirect manufacturing cost 間接製造成本
- indirect material 間接材料
- indirect production 間接生產
- indisputable fact 无可争辩的事实
- indisputable 无可争辩的,无可置疑的
- induce 引诱,劝诱,诱发
- inducement 引诱,诱惑,诱因
- induction training 就業訓練,入職訓練
- induction 引導
- indulge 寬容,纵容,延期付款

- indulgence　寬容,恩惠,縱容,特惠,付款延期
- industrial accident　工傷事故
- industrial conflict　勞資糾紛
- industrial dispute　勞資爭執,勞資糾紛,工業糾紛
- industrial diversification　工業多元化
- industrial goods　工業品
- industrial health and safety　工業衛生與安全
- industrial relations　勞資關係,工業關係
- industrial safety　工業安全
- industrial training　工業訓練
- industrial union　產業工會,工業工會
- industry　产业
- inequitable　不公正的,不公平的,偏私的
- infancy　未成年,幼年,嬰兒期
- infant industry　萌芽工業,初生工業,新興產業
- infanticide　杀害婴孩,杀婴(罪)
- inferior goods　劣等物品,低等物品
- infiltration　滲透
- inflation rate　通脹率
- inflation　通貨膨脹

- inflict death penalty 处以死刑
- informal organisation 非正式組織
- informant 告密者、綫人
- information management 資訊管理
- information processing 信息處理
- information system 信息系統,資訊系統
- information 正式起訴述
- informative advertising 資訊式廣告
- informed consent 知情的同意
- infraction 違規、違例
- infrastructure 基礎設施
- infringement of right 侵犯权利
- infringement 侵犯,违背,冒用商标,侵犯版权
- inherent 固有的,先天的,內在的,生来的
- inherent goodwill 內在商譽
- inherent right 固有權利
- inheritance of property 财产继承
- inheritance 繼承,遺產
- initial appearance 第一次出庭
- initial capital 創業資本

- initial cost 開辦費
- initial payment 首期付款
- injunction 禁令、強制令
- injuria 侵害,伤害,妨害权利
- injurious falsehood 伤害性的谎言
- injurious 有害的,伤害的,侮辱的,诽谤的
- injustice 不公正、不正義、不法
- inland, domestic 国内、国内的
- inmate 囚犯
- innovation 革新,改革,創新
- innuendo 影射,暗指,暗讽,注释
- input tax (VAT) 进项增值税
- input 投入,輸入,投入量
- input-output analysis 投入產出分析
- inquest 审讯,调查
- insane 精神病的,精神不正常
- insanity defense 精神失常辯護
- insanity 精神錯亂
- inseparability 生產與消費不可分割
- in-service training 在職訓練

- insider dealing　內幕交易
- insider trading　內幕交易
- insinuation　暗示,暗讽,间接讽刺,暗指
- insolvency　无力偿付债务,不足抵偿债务
- insolvent company　破产公司,无清偿债务能力的公司
- insolvent partner　無償債能力合夥人
- inspection of account　核阅帐目
- installment　分期付款
- installment credit　分期付款式賒帳,分期付款信貸
- installment loan　分期付款貸款
- installment sale　分期付款銷貨
- installment, partial payment　期款項、部分款項
- instigate　煽亂
- instruction　指示,訓令
- insult　侮辱,羞辱,无礼
- insurable interest　可保利益
- insurable risk　可保風險
- insurance　保险
- insurance coverage　承保范围,保险范围/项目
- insurance fraud　保險詐騙

- insurance fund　保險基金
- insurance policy　保單,保險單
- insurance premium　保費,保險費
- intake　落案
- intangibility　無形性
- intangible asset　無形資產
- intangible value　無形價值
- intangible　無形
- integration of enterprises　企業之整合
- integration　結合,合併
- integrity　忠誠廉潔
- intensive distribution　密集性分銷
- intention　意图,意向,蓄意,含义
- inter alia　其中包括,特別
- inter nos　在我们之间,不得外传
- inter se　在他们之间,在一组成员之间
- inter vivos　在世时,生前(赠与)
- inter-branch accounts　分店間往來帳
- inter-company profit　聯營公司間內部盈利
- inter-company transaction　聯營公司間交易事項

- intercourse 交往
- inter-departmental profit 部門間內部盈利
- interest 利息,權益,利益
- interest cap 利率差
- interest group 利益團體
- interest rate 利率
- interference 干预,妨碍
- interfirm comparison 公司間比較
- interim closing 中期結帳
- interim custody 临时拘留/押
- interim dividend 中期股息
- interim injunction 临时禁止令
- interim order 临时判令,临时裁决令
- interim payment 中期付款
- interim report 中期報告
- interlocking directors 互兼董事
- interlocutory 中期的,中間的
- intermittent production 間歇性生產
- internal audit 內部審計
- internal check 內部牽制,內部查核

- internal control system 內部控制系统
- internal control 內部管制,內部控制
- internal financing 內部融資
- internal transaction 內部會計事項
- internal transfer 內部調職
- international law 国际法
- international marketing 國際市場推銷
- international trade 國際貿易
- interpersonal skill 人際關係技能
- interplead (提出債權等要求者)相互诉讼
- interpleader 相互诉讼,互争权利的诉讼
- interpretation 解釋
- interpreter 口譯員
- interrogation [custodial] 盤問
- interstate 州際
- intestacy 未立遗嘱,无遗嘱的死亡
- intestate succession 无遗嘱继承(依法遗嘱)
- intestate's estate 无遗嘱的遗产
- intimacy 亲近/亲密的行为,熟悉,亲密,密切
- intimidation 恐嚇

- intoxication 酒醉，濫用禁藥
- intoxilizer 酒醉測試器
- intra vires 权限之内
- intrafirm comparison 公司內部比較
- intragroup indebtedness 集團內部負債
- intrinsic factor 內在因素
- intrinsic reward 內在報酬
- introduction stage 介紹期
- inventories 庫存
- inventory 存貨
- inventory control 存貨控制,存貨管理,存貨管制
- inventory cost 存貨成本
- inventory increase / decrease 庫存增/减变化
- inventory management 存貨管理
- inventory of property 财产目录,财产清册
- inventory turnover 存貨周轉,存貨流轉率
- invested capital 投入資本
- Investigation and Report (I&R) 調查與報告 (I&R)
- investigation 調查
- investment adviser 投資顧問

- investment appraisal　投資估價
- investment bank　投資銀行
- investment company　投資公司
- investment contract　投資契约/合同
- investment grant　投资补贴
- investment objective　投資目標
- investment portfolio　投資組合
- investment property　投资性房地产
- investor compensation fund　投資者賠償基金
- investor compensation regime　投資者賠償機制
- investor protection　投資者保障
- inviolability of property　财产(所有权)不可侵犯
- inviolable right　不可侵犯的权利
- invisible trade　無形貿易
- invoice　發票
- invoke　行使,援引,引起,恳求
- involuntary　非自愿的,非故意的,无意识的
- involuntary manslaughter　過失殺人
- ipso facto　根据事实本身,依事实
- ipso jure　依法律,根据法律

- irrational 不合理智的
- irreconcilable 难和解的,不能和解的,无法和解的
- irrecoverable 不能挽回的,不能弥补的,收不回的
- irredeemable stock 不可贖回股票
- irredeemable 不能赎回的,不能偿还的,不可兑现的
- irrelevant 不相干的,无关的,离题的
- irreparable damage 不可弥补的损失
- irretrievable 不能恢复的,无法挽救的
- irreversible 不可撤销的,不可改变的
- irrevocable condition 不可取消的条件
- irrevocable letter of credit 不可撤銷信用證
- irrevocable 不可撤销的,不可废除的
- issue 問題、爭論點,子女、後嗣
- to issue 發行、發出、分配
- issue a summons 发出传票
- issue in fact 事实上的争论点
- issue in law 法律上的争论点
- issued at a discount 折價發行
- issued at a premium 溢價發行
- issued at par 按面值發行

- issued capital　已發行股本
- issuing a bad check　簽發空頭支票
- itemize　列舉、詳細列舉

# J

- jail　　拘留所、監獄
- jailbreak　　越獄
- jay-walk　　違章穿越馬路
- job analysis　　工作分析,職務分析
- job attributes　　工作特質
- job characteristics　　工作特性
- job classification　　工作分類
- job content　　工作內容,工作質量
- job costing　　分批成本計演算法
- job description　　工作描述,工作說明,職務說明
- job design　　工作設計
- job enlargement　　工作擴大化
- job enrichment　　工作豐富化
- job evaluation　　工作評價
- job inspection　　實地視察工作情況
- job redesign　　工作再設計

- job rotation 工作輪調
- job satisfaction 工作滿足感
- job security 職業保障，工作保障
- job specification 工作規範,工作要求,職務規格
- job title 職銜
- jobber 證券經銷經紀,證券批銷經紀，批家
- joint 联合的,共同的,连带的,共同的,联接
- joint account 聯合帳
- joint action 共同诉讼,联合行动
- joint cost 聯合成本
- joint estate 共有财产
- joint lessee 共同承租人
- joint owners 共同所有权人,共同共有人,共有人
- joint ownership 共同所有權
- joint tenants 共同租借人
- joint venture 合營企業,合營項目,聯合短期投資
- jointly 共同,联合的,连带的
- journal 分錄簿,日記簿
- journal entry 日記分錄
- journalise 分錄

- joy riding   偷車兜風
- judge   法官
- Judge Advocate General   军法局长、军法处长
- judgement   判决,裁决
- judgement by default   缺席判决,缺席审判
- judgement creditor   判定债权人,胜诉债权人
- judgment debtor   判定债务人,败诉债务人
- judgment order   判决令
- judicature   司法权,审判制度,司法
- judicial   司法的
- judicial liquidation   法院判令的清盘
- judicial notice   司法上的认识,审判上的知识
- judicial officer   司法官员
- judicial precedent   司法判例,司法先例
- judicial proceedings   司法程序,审判程序
- judicial process   司法程序,审判程序,法院传票
- judicial separation   法庭裁定的分居
- judicial settlement   司法解决
- judicial system   司法制度
- judicial trustee   法定信托人,法定受托人

- judicial writ　法院令狀
- judiciary　司法系統
- jump bail　棄保潛逃
- junk dealer　收售舊物者
- jurisdiction　司法权,裁判权,审判权,管辖权
- jurisprudence　法理学,法学,法哲学
- jurist　法學家
- juror　陪審員
- juror, alternative　候補陪審員
- juror, prospective　待選陪審員
- juror, sworn　正選陪審員
- jury　陪審團
- jury box　陪審團席
- jury instructions　（法官給）陪審團的指示
- jury part　審判庭
- jury system　陪审制度
- jury tempering　非法干預陪審團
- jury trial　陪審團審案
- just　公正的,正当的,正义的,正直的,公平的
- just cause　正当理由,合法理由

- justice 公正,正义,公平,公道
- justification 理由正当,合法理由,辨明
- juvenile 少年
- juvenile court 少年法庭
- juvenile delinquency 少年违法犯罪,少年犯罪
- juvenile delinquent 青少年/未成年人罪犯
- juvenile offender 少年犯

# K

- kerb   路堤
- key   主要的,基本的,钥匙
- key executive insurance   關鍵管理人員保險
- key personnel   主要工作人員
- key witness   主要证人
- kidnap   诱拐,绑架,拐带,绑票
- kidnapping   綁架、綁票
- killer   兇手
- kiting   開空頭支票
- kiting cheque   空頭支票
- kleptomania   盜竊狂
- know-how   诀窍
- knowingly   知情地、故意地
- knowledge   认识,知识
- known liability   已知負債
- known loss   已知損失

# L

- labeling  標籤
- labor law  勞工法、勞動法
- Labour Department  勞工處
- labour dispute  勞資爭議,勞資糾紛
- labour force  勞動力,勞動人口
- labour intensive  勞力密集型
- labour market  勞動市場,勞動力市場
- labour mobility  勞工流動性
- Labour Relations Ordinance  勞資關係條例
- labour relations  勞資關係
- Labour Tribunal  勞資審裁處
- labour turnover rate  勞工流動率,員工流動率
- labour union  工會,職工會
- laceration  裂伤
- lag  延遲
- laissez faire  自由放任

- land and building 房地產
- land transport authority 陆路交通管理局
- land 土地,陆地,国土
- landed property 不动产,地产
- landed 不动产的,有土地的
- landmark decision 里程碑式的判决
- larceny 盗竊罪
- large-scale enterprise 大型企业
- Last-In-First-Out (LIFO) 後進先出法
- late payment fine 逾期罚金、滞纳罚金
- latent demand 潛在需求,潛在需要
- latent prints 隱藏的指印
- lateral communication 橫向溝通
- laterite road 红土路
- law 法律,法令,定律,规律
- law code 法典、法例
- law enforcement agency 執法機構
- law firm 律師事務所
- law guardian 法律監護人
- law of contract 契约法,合同法

- law of damages　损害赔偿法
- law of equity　衡平法
- law of evidence　证据法
- law of large number　大數法則
- law of procedure　诉讼法,诉讼程序法
- law of restitution　赔偿法
- law school　法學院
- lawful excuse　合法理由
- lawful impediment　合法障碍
- lawful means　合法手段,合法途径
- lawful measures　合法措施
- lawful son　合法儿子
- lawsuit　官司、訴訟、案件
- lawyer, attorney　律师
- layoff　遣散
- lead council　首席律師
- leadership　領導能力
- leadership style　領導風格
- leadership traits　領導特徵
- leading　領導

- leading question 引导性讯问,诱导性讯问
- lease 租賃,租,租約
- lease contract 租赁合同
- lease term 租期
- leasehold improvements 租入资产改良
- leasehold 租赁权,租赁期
- leasing 租賃
- leave 准许,许可,同意,假期,休假,告别
- leave of absence 请准休假,假释
- leave to defend 准许辩护,批准答辩
- lechery 淫亂行爲
- ledger 分類帳
- ledger control 分類帳統制,分類帳控制
- legacy 遺產
- legal age 法定年龄
- legal aid bureau 法律援助局
- legal aid 法律援助
- legal consequences 法律后果
- legal council 法律顧問
- legal counseling 法律咨询

- legal currency   法定货币
- legal custody   合法拘留,法定监禁,法定监护
- legal draftsman   法案草拟人,法案撰拟人
- legal entity   法人,法定個體,合法組織
- legal estate   法定产权,合法财产(权)
- legal force   法律效力
- legal incapacity   无法律上的行为能力
- legal language   法律语言,法律用语
- legal liability   法律责任
- legal matter (s)   法律事件,法律问题
- legal maxim   法律格言,法律谚语,法律准则
- legal notice   法律通告,法律通知,法律告示
- legal obligation   法律義務
- legal officer   政府
- legal precedent   判例
- legal procedure   法律程序,法定程序
- legal proceedings   法律诉讼(程序),法定程序
- legal provision   法律规定,法律条文
- legal redress   法律(上的)补偿,法律(上的)赔偿
- legal representative   法定代表,法定代理人

- legal reserve    法定留存、准备、公积金
- legal restraint    合法限制,法律约束
- legal right    法定权利,合法权利
- legal sanction    法律制裁,法律认可
- legal step    法定手续
- legal supplement    法律附则,法律补遗
- legal system    法制,法律体系,法律制度
- legal tender    法定货币
- legal terms    法律名词,法律术语
- legal time    法定时间
- legal title    法定所有权,合法所有权
- legal, statutory    法定的、法律上的、合法的
- legalese    法律術語
- legality    合法性
- legality of arrest    拘捕合法
- legation    公使馆,使节的派遣
- legislate    立法,制定法律
- legislation    立法,法规,法制,制定法
- legislator    立法委员,议员
- legitimacy    合法,合法性,婚生

- legitimate child 婚生子女
- legitimate 合法的,合理的,正当的
- legitimate power 合法權力
- legitimate self-defence 合法自卫,正当自卫
- length of service 服務年資
- leniency 宽待,宽厚,仁慈,从轻发落
- lessee 承租人,租户,租用人,租地人
- lesser included charge 包括的較輕指控
- lesser included offense 包括的較輕控罪
- lessor 出租人,租主,业主
- lethal injection 致命性注射劑
- lethal weapon 致命兇器
- letter bomb 信件炸彈
- letter of appointment 聘書
- letter of credit 信用證,信用狀
- letter of credit 信用证
- letter of disposition 結案證書
- letter of enquiry 詢價函件
- letter of patent 专利证书
- letter of procuration 委任狀

- letters of inheritance  继承书
- level of management  管理層次,管理階層
- level of responsibility  責任的輕重
- level of salary  薪金水平
- leverage  挺率,槓率,槓杆比率,資本借貸率
- levy  征收,征税,抽税,强索,征集,扣押
- lewd conduct  猥褻行爲、淫穢行爲、下流行爲
- liabilities  债务、负债
- liability insurance  責任保險
- liability loss  責任損失
- liable  有(法律)责任的,有义务的
- libel  誹謗罪
- licence  执照,许可,特许,认可,许可证,特许证
- licensed bank  持牌銀行
- licensed deposit taking company  持牌接受存款公司
- lie in wait  埋伏以待
- life assurance  人壽保險
- life imprisonment  终生監禁,无期徒刑
- life insurance  人寿保险
- life sentence  無期徒刑、終生監禁

- lift landing 电梯平台,上下电梯的地方,电梯口
- limit of time 时效
- limited 有限的
- limited company 有限公司
- limited liability company law 有限責任公司法
- limited liability 有限債務責任,有限責任
- limited means 经济能力有限,有限方法
- limited partner 有限合夥人
- line assistant 直線助理,部屬助理
- line authority 直線職權,部屬職權
- line function 直線功能,部屬功能,直線職能
- line manager 作業主管
- line of authority 權力線
- line organization 直線組織,部屬組織
- line-and-staff organisation 直線與幕僚組織
- lineup 列隊辨認嫌疑犯
- linked exchange rate 聯繫匯率
- liquid asset 速動資產,流動資產
- liquid capital 流動資金
- liquid funds 流动资金

- liquidated damages 协定的损害赔偿金
- liquidation of debt 清还债务
- liquidation 清盘,收盘,清算,清偿
- liquidator 清盘人,清算人
- liquidity 流動性,變現性,變現能力
- liquidity ratio 速動比率,流動資金比率
- listed company 上市公司
- listed security 上市證券
- listing requirement 上市條件
- listing rules 上市規則
- litigant 诉讼当事人,诉讼的
- litigate 訴訟
- litigation 訴訟、打官司
- litigious right 诉讼权利
- live ammunition 實彈
- loaded weapon 裝上彈藥的武器
- loading charge 裝船費用
- loan 放款,貸款
- loan capital 借貸資本,借入資本
- loan interest 貸款利息

- loan shark　高利貸者
- loan stock　債券
- loans, bonds　借款，债券
- lobbying　遊說
- local currency　本地货币
- local supervision　地方監管
- localisation of production　生產地方化
- location of industry　工業區位,選址
- lockout　停工,工廠閉鎖
- locus standi　言权,出庭资格,正式地位,陈述权
- lodge　提出(申诉等),提呈,呈交,寄宿
- lodge a complaint　控告,投訴
- lodgement　提出,告发,控告,住所,住宿
- lodgement in court　向法庭提出的起诉,向法院起诉
- lodgement of document　提呈文件
- logistics　物流服務
- loitering　闲荡 閑蕩
- long-term　长期
- long-term financing　長期籌資
- long-term capital　長期資本,長期資金

- long-term contract　長期合約
- long-term investment　長期投資
- long-term lease　長期租賃
- long-term liability　長期負債
- long-term loan　長期貸款
- lookout [for a sale]　把風
- loophole　漏洞
- looting　洗劫、趁亂打劫
- loss　损失,丧失,遗失,亏损,伤亡,损毁,浪费
- loss leader　虧本出售商品,招徠性商品,特價商品
- loss of possession　占有权的丧失
- loss ratio　損失比率
- low geared　低資本借貨比率
- low value fixed assets　低值固定资产
- lower of cost or market　成本與市價孰低法
- LSD　迷幻藥
- lump-sum　總額,整筆
- lynching　私刑處死

# M

- macroeconomic control policy　宏觀調控政策
- Mafia　黑手黨、黑社會
- magistrate　裁判官
- magistrate's complaint　向推事所作的投訴
- magistrate's court　推事庭,推事法庭
- mail bomb　郵件炸彈
- mail fraud　郵件欺詐
- mail order　郵購
- mail theft　郵件盜竊
- maiming　殘害
- main board　第一版市場,主板市場
- maintenance　生活費,維持
- maintenance costs　維修費
- maintenance expense　維修成本
- maintenance of justice　維護正義,維持公道
- maintenance reserve　維修準備

- major offence　重罪,主要罪行
- majority　多数,大多数,半数以上,成年,法定成年
- majority verdict　多数裁决
- make out one's case　证明自己有理由
- making arrest　拘捕、逮捕
- malefactor　作恶者
- malfeasance　渎职(罪),不法行为,滥用职权
- malfeasant　渎职的,非法行为的,违法乱纪者
- malice　恶意
- malicious　恶意的,存心不良的,蓄意的,有敌意的
- malicious intention　恶意,犯罪意图
- malicious mischief　恶意作弄
- malicious prosecution　恶意控告,诬告,恶意检控
- malign　污蔑、詆毁
- malpractice　不正当的行为,渎职,营私舞弊
- maltreatment　虐待,粗暴对待
- management　管理,治理,管理部門,管理階層
- management accounting　管理會計
- management board　企业管理层
- management bonus　经理、董事红利

- management by exception 例外管理
- management consultant 管理顧問,經營顧問
- management contract 管理合約
- management development 管理發展
- management efficiency 管理效能
- management function 管理功能
- management game 管理遊戲
- Management Information System (MIS) 管理資訊系統
- management level 管理階層
- management principle 管理原則
- management report 管理报告
- management science 管理科學
- management skill 管理技能
- management structure 管理機構
- manager 經理,管理者,管理人員
- managerial hierarchy 管理層次,管理結構
- managing director 常務董事
- mandamus 命令狀,训令,指令,执行令
- mandate 執行令
- mandatory minimum sentence 法定最低刑期

- mandatory sentences 規定死期
- mandatory surcharge 法定庭費
- mandatory 規定的、強制性的
- manhunt 搜捕逃犯
- manipulation of data 操縱資訊
- manner of payment 付款方式
- manpower planning 人力規畫,人力計畫
- manslaughter 過失殺人、誤殺
- manufacturing account 製造帳戶
- manufacturing costs 制造成本,生产成本
- manufacturing enterprise 製造企業
- manufacturing operation 製造業
- manufacturing overhead 製造費用
- margin 毛利
- margin of safety 安全邊際
- marginal balance 獲利差額
- marginal contribution to profit 邊際利潤貢獻
- marginal costing 邊際成本法,邊際成本計算
- Marijuana 大麻,草
- marine insurance 海上保險,水險

- marital rights  婚姻权,夫权
- maritime law  海事法,海商法
- mark-down  標價降低數,減成
- marked money [to buy]  有記認[購買]紙幣
- market analysis  市道分析,市場分析
- market capitalization  市值,市價總值
- market development  市場發展
- market diversification  市場多元化,市場分散
- market economy  市場經濟
- market information  行情,市場信息
- market leader  市場領導者
- market manipulation  市場操縱
- market mechanism  市場調節作用,市場調節職能
- market niche  市場空間
- market orientation  市場導向,市場取向
- market penetration  市場滲透
- market potential  市場潛力
- market price  市價
- market research/marketing research  市場研究
- market segmentation  市場細分,市場區隔化

- market value 市值
- market volume 市場容量
- marketable security 有價證券
- marketing 銷售,推銷,市場營銷,市場推廣
- marketing concept 市場觀念,市場營銷概念
- marketing decision 市場決策,營銷決策
- marketing effort 市場效能,營銷效能
- marketing environment 市場環境,行銷環境
- marketing function 市務職能
- marketing information system 市場資料系統
- marketing management 市場管理,市務管理
- marketing mix 市場組合,行銷組合,市場營運組合
- marketing policy 市場政策,營銷政策
- marketing strategy 市場策略,營銷策略
- mark-up 成本加成,加於成本之價格,標價提高數
- marriage 婚姻,结婚,婚姻生活,结合
- married woman 已婚妇女,有夫之妇
- marshal 髮精、庭警
- martial law 军法,军事统制法,戒严法令
- mass distribution 大規模運銷

- mass hysteria 集體發瘋
- mass production 大量生產,大規模生產
- matching concept 相配觀念, 配比概念
- material 重要的,实质性的,决定性的,本质的
- material alteration 重大修改,实质性变更
- material cost 材料成本
- material evidence 重要的证据,实质性证据,物证
- material facts 重要事實
- material incentive 物質鼓勵
- material management 物料管理
- material statement 重要聲明
- material witness 重要證人
- materiality 重要性, 重點鉅數
- maternity leave 分娩假期,產假
- mate's receipt 大副收據
- matrimonial property 婚姻所有财产
- matrimony 婚姻,结婚,婚礼
- matrix departmentalisation 矩陣分部
- matrix organisation 矩陣組織
- matter(s) of fact 事实上的问题,事实上

- matter of record   有案可查的事項
- matter(s)   事件,事情,事項,事務,问题,物质
- maturity   到期,成熟期
- maturity date   到期日,期满日
- maxim   格言,准则,箴言
- maximum sentence   最高刑罚
- maximum stock level   最高存貨水平
- mayhem   殘害身體
- mean   平均值,中數
- meaning   意义,意思,含义
- means of defence   辩护方法,防御手段
- means of production   生產工具,生產方式
- means of proof   证明方法,举证方法
- means of subsistence   维持生计方法,生计
- means   方法,方式,经济状况／能力,手段,资力
- measure(s)   措施,方法,量度,程度,限度,估计
- mechanisation   機械化
- median   中位數
- mediation   調停、仲裁
- mediation-arbitration   调解-仲裁

- medical examination 体格检查,医生检查
- medical examiner 法醫
- medical scheme 醫療計畫
- medium-sized enterprise 中型企業
- memorandum 备忘录,摘要,便函
- menacing 人身威嚇
- mens rea 犯罪意图,犯意
- mental disease/defect 精神疾病或缺陷
- mental incapacity 精神上無能為力量
- mental patient 精神病人
- mentally ill 精神上有病
- mention in court 过堂
- mention 举述,提及,提到,说起
- mentoring 顧問指導
- mercantile law 商法
- merchandise 商品,貨品
- merchant bank 商人銀行
- merchant wholesaler 批發商
- merchantable quality 適合銷售品質,可銷售品質
- mercy 怜悯,宽恕,慈悲,仁慈

- merger 兼併,合併,歸併
- merit rating system 人事考績制度,人事考核制度
- merits of the case 案情有利点
- middle manager 中層管理人員
- middleman 中間人
- mid-term 中期
- migration date 移居日期
- military court 军事法庭
- military law 军法,军事法
- mind 思想,心意,精神,智力,头脑
- minimum sentence 最低刑罚
- minimum standard 最低標準
- minimum stock level 最低存貨水平
- minimum wage 最低工资
- minor injury 轻伤
- minor offence 轻微罪行,轻罪
- minor 未成年的,较轻微的,较次要的
- minority 少数,少数票
- minority balance 少數差額
- minority interest 少數股東權益

- minority shareholders   少数股东
- misadventure   意外事故,横祸
- misapplication of property   濫用財產
- misappropriation   濫用,侵吞,不正當使用
- misbehaviour   不正当的举止,行为不良,举止失检
- miscarriage   误送,小产,流产
- miscarriage of justice   审判不公,误判,审判不当
- miscellaneous expense   雜費
- mischief   恶作剧,损害,伤害,危害
- mischief by fire   纵火恶作剧
- misconceive   误解,有错误看法
- misconception   误解,看法错误
- misconduct   不法行爲、不端行爲
- misdemeanor   不端行为,不轨行为,行为失检
- misleading question   誤導問題
- misleading statement   误导性的供述
- misnomer   誤稱
- misquote   錯誤引用
- missing   失蹤
- mistrial   無效審判（可重審）

- misuse of credit 信貸濫用
- misuse of fund 資金誤用
- mitigating circumstances 減罪細節
- mitigating factors 減罪因素
- mitigation 缓和
- mixed account 混合帳戶
- mixed departmentalisation 混合分部
- mobile shop 流動商店
- mode 模式,方式,形式
- mode of payment 付款方式
- mode of trial 审讯方式
- modernisation 现代化
- modus 方法,方式,手段
- modus operandi 作案惯技,干案手法,办事方法
- molest 非礼
- monetary detrimental 经济上的损害
- monetary fine, penalty 罚金、罚款
- monetary system 貨幣制度
- money 钱
- money laundering 洗錢

- money market 貨幣市場
- money measurement concept 貨幣量度單位觀念
- money order 匯票
- monogamous marriage 一夫一妻制婚姻
- monogamy 一夫一妻制
- monopolist 壟斷者,
- monopoly 垄断,独占,专利事业,专卖(权)
- moot 假設的、非實際的
- moral certainty 確實可靠性
- moral standard 道德標準
- moral turpitude 卑鄙 違背道德、卑鄙
- morale 士氣
- mortgage bond 抵押債券
- mortgage 抵押
- mortgaged property 已抵押的财产
- mortgagor 抵押者,借款人
- motion 動議
- motion denied 動議被否決
- motion granted 動議被批准
- motion study 動作研究

- motion to dismiss　撤消動議
- motivation　激勵
- motivational factor/motivator　動機因子, 激勵因子
- motive　動機
- movable property　动产
- mug shot　入案照片
- multinational corporation　跨國公司, 多國公司
- multiple pricing　多重訂價法
- multiple shop　連鎖商店
- muniments of title　产权证书
- murder　谋杀(罪)
- murder in the first degree　一等谋杀
- murder in the second degree　二等谋杀
- murderer　谋杀犯, 凶手
- mutatis mutandis　细节上作必要的修正
- mute　故意不答辩的, 缄默无言, 哑的
- mutilation　切斷、殘害、毀傷
- mutiny　兵變、叛變
- mutual　相互的, 共同的, 彼此的
- mutual aid　互助

- mutual consent  双方同意
- mutual fund  互惠基金,共同基金
- mutually exclusive projects  互斥项目

# N

- narcotics 麻醉品
- narrative 摘要,說明
- national income 國民所得,國民收入
- nationalisation 國有化
- native-born citizen 土生公民
- natural child 非亲生子女,私生子女
- natural death 自然死亡,正常死亡
- natural evidence 自然证据
- natural father 生父
- natural resources 天然資源
- natural right(s) 自然权利,生而具有的权利
- naturalization 入境、歸化
- nearside 左边
- necessity 必需品
- need for achievement 成就感需要
- need for affiliation 歸屬感需要

- need for power　權力需要
- need hierarchy　需要層次
- negative goodwill　負商譽
- neglect　疏忽,疏漏,忽略,玩忽,弃置不顾
- neglect of duty　失职,忽略责任,玩忽职守
- negligence　疏忽、過失
- negligence of duty　疏忽職守
- negligent driving　疏忽驾驶
- negligent homicide　過失殺人
- negligent manslaughter　過失殺人
- negligent　疏忽的,玩忽的,过失的
- negotiable　可转让的,可流通的,可谈判的
- negotiable instrument　可轉讓票據,流通票據
- negotiation　谈判
- nepotism　任人唯親、裙帶風
- net　淨價
- net asset value　資產淨值
- net book value　帳面淨值
- net current asset　流動資產淨值
- net income　淨利益,淨收益,淨利,純利

- net loss 淨損失
- net loss for the year 年度亏损
- net operating income 營業淨利
- net operating profit 營業淨利
- net proceed 淨收入
- net profit 純利,淨利
- net profit on sales 銷貨純利
- net purchases 購貨淨額
- net realisable value 可变现净值
- net sales 銷貨淨額
- net sales proceeds 销售净收入
- net sales, turnover 销售收入
- net value 净值
- net working capital 營運資金淨額
- net worth 淨值
- network 网络
- neutrality law 中立法
- new issue market 新股發行市場
- new product development 新產品發展
- next of kin 最近親屬

- nisi   除非,不然则,非最后的,非绝对的
- no claim bonus   無索償獎勵,無賠償記錄獎金
- no contest   無爭議
- no true bill   不與起訴, 不以起訴
- nolle prosequi   不起訴
- nolo contendere   不辯不認
- nominal   票额的,名义上的,象征性的
- nominal account   損益帳戶,名義帳戶
- nominal capital   票面股本,額定股本,名義股本
- nominal damages   象征式赔偿(金),名义上的损害赔偿
- nominal partner   名義合夥人
- nominal punishment   象征式处分,象征性处罚
- nominal rate of return   名義回報率
- nominal value   名義價值,票面值
- nomination   提名,任命,委任,指定,推荐
- nominee   获提名者,受任命者,受任者,被指定者
- non est factum   否认订立合同／契约的答辩
- non prosequitur   不追诉
- non sequitur   不根据前提而作出的推断
- non tenure   否认占有

- non  不,非
- non-adjusting event  非調整事項
- non-contributory provident fund  毋須供款的公積金
- non-cumulative preference share  非累積優先股
- non-durable goods  非耐用品
- non-executive director  非執行董事
- nonfeasance  不履行義務
- non-financial incentive  非財務式獎勵
- non-insurable risk  不可保風險
- non-operating expenses (income)  营业外支出(收入)
- non-operating  非營業
- non-payment  不支付、未繳納
- non-profit making organization  非牟利機構
- non-programmed decision  非定型化決策
- non-resident taxpayer  境外纳税人
- nonresident  非（某地）居民
- non-support of a child  不撫養子女
- non-voting share  無投票權股票
- no-par-value capital stock  無面值股票
- not guilty  無罪

- not negotiable　不得轉讓
- notary public　公證人
- note　票據
- notes payable　应付票据
- notes receivable　应收票据
- to notice　通知,注意,布告,声明,通告,告示
- notice　通知書，通知
- notice of appeal　上訴通知書
- notice of defence　辩护通知书,答辩通知书
- notice of question　质询通知书,提出问题的通知
- notice of termination　期满通知,终止(合同)通知书
- notice of trial　审讯通知(书)
- notice of withdrawal　取消通知(书),撤销诉讼通知
- notice　通知,注意,布告,声明,通告,告示
- noting charge　票據拒付手續費
- nuisance　妨害公共利益的行爲
- null　无束缚力的,无效的,作废的
- null and void　無效、失效
- nullification　无效,废弃,取消,废止
- nullify　取消

- nullity 无效,作废
- nullity of contract 无效契约,无效合同
- nullity of marriage 婚姻无效,无效婚姻

# O

- oath  誓言
- oath of allegiance  宣誓效忠
- obiter dictum  (法官的)附带意见,附论
- objection  反對、抗議、異議
- objectivity  客觀性
- obligation  負債,責任
- obnoxious matter(s)  应受处罚的事件,应受谴责的
- obscene  猥褻的,诲淫的,污秽的,淫猥的
- obscenity  猥褻、淫穢、下流
- obsolescence  陳廢,過時,陳舊
- obstruct  阻碍,妨碍,阻挠
- obstructing justice  妨害司法
- occupancy  占据,据有,占有,占用,占有期间
- occupant  占有者,占用者,居住者,居用者
- occupation, profession  专业、职业
- occupation, self-employed  自雇职业
- occupational mobility  職業流動性

- occupier's liability　住户的责任,住用者的责任
- odd lot　零數,零星交易,零星股,碎股
- odd pricing　奇數定價法
- offence against the law　违法行为
- offend　触犯,违犯,犯罪,犯法,伤害
- offender　罪犯,冒犯者,犯罪者,犯法者
- offense　罪行、犯法
- offensive　冒犯的,侮辱的,攻击性的,令人反感
- offensive exhibition　不文露體
- offensive language　无礼的话,令人反感的言语
- offensive weapon　攻击性武器
- offer for sale　公開發售,出讓
- office furniture and equipment　办公家具及设备
- office supplies　办公用品
- officer　政府官员 / 人员
- official communication　官方公文,正式照会
- official misconduct　官員瀆職
- official receiver　官方产业接管人
- official trustee　官方信托人,官方受托人
- offset　抵銷,沖銷

- offside 右边
- off-the-job training 職外訓練
- oligopoly 寡頭壟斷
- on account 賒帳
- on credit 賒帳
- on demand 見票即付
- on hand 手存
- on the record 記錄在案
- on trial 在审,受审
- one way communication 單向溝通
- onerous property 负有义务的财产
- onus of proof 提出证据的责任,举证责任
- open account 欠帳,未清帳戶
- open book account 往來賒欠帳戶
- open cheque 無劃線支票,現金支票,現金票
- open question 未决问题,待决的问题
- open verdict 悬案,死因未详的裁决
- opening balance 期初餘額
- opening entry 開帳分錄
- opening statement 開案陳述/陳詞

- operating　業務上
- operating company　營業公司
- operating cost　營業成本,營運成本
- operating cycle　營業循環
- operating expense　營業費用
- operating income　營業收益
- operating lease　经营租赁
- operating leverage　營業槓杆
- operating profit　營業收益,營業利潤
- operating ratio　營業比率
- operating segment　经营分部
- operational planning　運作規畫
- operations management　營運管理
- opinion leader　意見領袖
- opportunism　機會主義
- opportunity cost　機會成本
- option dealing　期權買賣
- oral discussion　口头讨论
- oral examination　口头审问,口试
- order　命令,訂貨,訂貨單,訂單

- order cheque  記名支票,抬頭支票
- order of acquittal  无罪释放令
- order of attachment  扣押令
- order of committal  拘禁令
- order of discharge  解除破产令,撤销令,解除令
- order of exemption  豁免令
- order of mandamus  履行责任令
- order of payment  付款凭单
- order of protection  保護令
- order point  訂購點
- ordering cost  訂購成本
- ordinance  法令、條例
- ordinary share  普通股
- organisation chart  組織圖表,組織圖
- organisation design  組織設計
- organisation development  組織發展
- organisation structure  組織結構
- organisational climate  組織氣氛,組織氣候
- organized crime  有組織犯罪
- orientation  新員工輔導,職前輔導,職前訓練

- original cost　原始成本
- original entry　原始分錄
- originating summons　引发诉讼传票
- ostensible partner　掛名合夥人
- ostentatious goods　炫耀性物品
- ostracism　排斥
- outgoing partner　退出合夥人,退夥人
- outlaw　歹徒
- to outlaw　取締、剝奪（權利）
- outlay　支出
- output　產量，產出,輸出
- output device　輸出設備,輸出裝置
- outstanding　未清的,未清還的
- outstanding capital contributions　未缴入股额
- outstanding cheque　未兌現支票
- outstanding expense　未付費用
- outstanding liability　未付負債,未還清負債
- outstanding warrant　未執行的逮捕證
- over act　明顯/公開行爲
- overcast　多計

- overdraft credit, open credit  帐户透支款项
- overdraft  透支
- overdue  逾期
- overhaul expense  大修理費用
- overhead  間接費用,經常費用
- overrule  駁回、推翻
- overstatement  多列,多計
- oversubscription  超額認購
- overtaking dangerously  危险超车
- over-the-counter trading  場外交易,直接交易
- over-the-counter  場外的
- over-the-counter-market  場外交易市場
- overtime  加班工时
- over-trading  過度擴張營運,營業超荷
- overvaluation  計價過高
- owe  欠
- owner  拥有人,物主,所有权人
- owner's equity  資本主權,業主權益
- ownership utility  所有權效用
- ownership  所有权,拥有权,所有制

# P

- paper money    纸币
- paper profit    帳面盈餘
- par value    票面值,面值
- pari passu    公平地,平等地,同等地,以相等的比量
- parole    假釋
- parole revocation    撤消假釋
- parole supervision    假釋監管
- parole violation    違反假釋
- part payment    部分付款,部分支付
- part performance    部分 / 局部履行
- partial incapacity    局部喪失能力
- partial loss    局部损失,部分损失
- partial verdict    部分裁决
- participating preferred stock    參與優先股
- participation, investment    參股、投资
- participative management    參與式管理,參與管理

- partnership 合夥,合夥組織,合夥企業
- party 當事人
- pass judgment 作判决,宣判
- pass sentence 宣判刑罚
- passport 护照,通行证
- past due 逾期
- patent law, patent right 专利法,专利权
- patent 专利权,专利证,专卖权,显著的
- paternity suit 確認生父的訴訟
- to pay 付清,偿还,支付,工资,报酬,报偿
- pay by instalment 分期付款
- pay grade 薪酬等級
- pay in advance 预付,预缴
- pay plan 薪酬計畫
- pay scale 薪級
- payable 应付款项
- payback method 歸本期方法
- payback period 還本期,歸本年期,回收期
- payee 受款人,收款人
- payer 付款人

- payment     支付,付款,付款额,支付款项
- payment by installment     分期付款
- payment in advance     預付
- payment in arrear     積欠
- payment in full     全部付清
- payment in lieu     付款代替
- payment notice     付款通知
- payroll     工资单
- pecuniary     金钱的,应罚款的
- pecuniary donation     金钱捐赠,捐款
- pecuniary legacy     金钱遗赠
- pecuniary loss     金钱损失,经济损失
- pecuniary offence     应罚款的违法行为,应科罚金的罪
- pecuniary punishment     罚款处分,科以罚款的处分
- pegged exchange rate system     掛鈎匯率制
- penal jurisprudence     刑法学
- penal law     刑法
- penal practice     刑罚程序
- penal provision     刑罚条款,刑法规定
- penal sentence     徒刑,刑事判决

- penal statute　刑事法令
- penal treatment　刑罚处分,刑事处分
- penalty　惩罚,处罚,刑罚
- pending matter(s)　悬搁事项,未决事项
- pending trial　候审,待审
- penitentiary　監獄
- pension　退休金
- pension accrual　退休准备金
- pension fund　撫恤基金，退休基金
- pension scheme　長俸計畫,長俸制度
- per dim　按日津貼
- per incuriam　因疏忽,因失察
- per infortunium　失误,意外之失
- per　经,由,靠,每,按,依,通过,因
- percentage profit　利潤比率
- percentage statement　百分率比較表
- performance　清偿,履行,执行,完成,行为,行动
- performance appraisal　員工考績,工作評核
- performance management　表現管理
- performance of debt　债务清偿

- performance test　有績效測驗,性能試驗
- period cost　期間成本
- periodic inventory system 分期盤點制,定期盤存制
- perishability　易逝性
- perjured witness　作伪证者,作假证的证人
- perjury　伪证(罪),伪誓,发假誓
- permanent　具永久性,永远的,长期的,不变的
- permanent resident　永久居民
- perpetrator　作案者、肇事者
- perpetual inventory system　永續盤存制
- persistent felony offender　一貫的重罪犯
- persistent sexual abuse　持續的性虐待
- personal account　人名帳戶,個人往來帳戶
- personal budget　個人財務預算
- personal characteristic　个人特征
- personal credit record　個人信貸紀錄
- personal finance　個人財物管理
- personal financial management　個人理財
- personal financial situation　個人財務狀況
- personal income　個人所得,個人收入

- personal injury claim　人身伤害的索偿
- personal liability　個人責任,個人負債
- personal property　動產,個人財產
- personal selling　人員銷售,個人銷售
- personal violence　个人暴行
- personalised product　個人化產品
- personalised service　個人化服務
- personality test　人格測驗,性格測驗
- personnel expenses　劳务费用
- personnel loss　員工流失
- personnel management　人事管理
- persuasive advertising　誘導性廣告
- persuasive precedent　有说服力的判例
- petition　申请(书),请愿(书),请求,祈求,诉状
- petition for probate　申请遗嘱验证
- petition of mercy　请求赦免书,赦免请求书
- petition of right(s)　权利请愿书 / 申请书
- petition the court　向法庭請願
- petitioner　请愿人,申请人,呈请人,诉愿人
- petty cash book　零用現金簿

- petty cash voucher　零用現金憑單
- petty theft　小偷
- physical count (inventory)　实地盘点、实物盘存
- physical distribution　實體配銷
- physical need　生理需要
- physical possession　实质占有,物质占有
- physical stock taking　實地盤點,實地盤存
- physiological need　生存需要,生理需要
- picket line　警戒綫、糾察綫
- piece rate　件薪,按件計酬,計件工資(率)
- piecemeal distribution　分期分配
- piecemeal realisation　分期變現,分期變產
- piece-work wage　计件工资
- piracy　盜版
- pistol　手槍
- place of detention　拘留所
- place utility　地方效用
- placement　安置,崗位安置
- plaintiff　原告
- plant and equipment　廠房與設備

- plausibility check    可行性檢查
- plea    應辯/答辯
- plea agreement    認罪協議
- plea and (in) abeyance    暫停答辯
- plea bargain    認罪求情、認罪協議
- plea of guilty by post    通过邮件方式认罪
- plea of guilty    认罪,表示认罪
- plea of mitigation    请求从轻发落
- plead for leniency    恳求宽容治罪,请求从轻刑罚
- plead guilty    認罪答辯
- plead guilty to a charge    認罪
- plead innocent/not guity    無罪答辯
- pleading    诉状,答辩书,诉讼文书
- pledge    抵押
- pledging accounts receivable    應收帳款抵押
- plight    誓約、困境
- plunder    掠奪品
- to plunder    搶劫、掠奪
- police    警察,警察当局,警方人员
- police car    巡邏車

- police detail　警察特定任務對
- police dispatcher　警察調度員
- police dog　警犬
- police power　警方权力
- police precinct　警察局
- police record　警察紀錄
- policy　政策,方針，保險單,保單
- policy holder　保險客戶,投保人
- policy matter(s)　政策問題
- political skill　政治能力
- polluting　污染
- polyandry　一妻多夫制
- polygamy　一夫多妻制
- pornographer　製作色情作品的人
- pornographic material　色情材料
- pornography　色情
- portfolio　投資組合,證券組合，資產組合
- port-of-entry　入境口岸
- portside　左边,左舷
- position statement　資產負債表,財務狀況表

- positioning 定位
- possess 占有,擁有,持有,具有
- possession of gambling records 持有賭博記錄
- possession of narcotics 持有麻醉品
- possession utility 所有權效用
- possessor 持有人,占有人,所有者,擁有者
- possessory right(s) 占有权
- post balance sheet event 資產負債表後事項
- post/make bail 具保
- post-acquisition profit or loss 收購後損益
- postal communication service 郵遞通訊服務
- post-closing balance sheet 結帳後平衡帳
- post-closing trial balance 結帳後試算表
- post-dated cheque 期票,遠期支票
- posting 過帳
- postpurchase behavior 購買後行為
- postpurchase satisfaction 購買後滿足感
- potential anlaysis 潛力分析
- potential customer 潛在主顧,潛在顧客
- pound 兽栏 獸欄

- power charge 動力費用
- power of attorney 委托書、授權書、代理書
- power of procuration 委任权
- practice 专业,业务,诉讼程序,实践,实行,惯例
- practice of advocacy 律师业务
- practise law 执律师业
- practising certificate 执业证书,执业执照
- praecipe 原令状,致法院的申请便笺
- prank 惡作劇
- pre- investigation 判刑前調查
- pre- report 判刑前報告
- pre-acquisition profit or loss 收購前損益
- preamble 序文,序言,导言,绪言
- precaution 預防(措施),警惕
- precedence 优先,领先,在前,优先权
- precedent 先例,判例,在前的,在先的,优先的
- pre-closing trial balance 結帳前試算表
- predicate felony offender 有前科的重罪犯
- prediction 預測
- preemptive right 優先認購股權,優先認股權

- preemptory challenge　不述理由而要求陪審員退席
- preference share dividend　優先股利,優先股股息
- preference share premium　優先股利，優先股溢價
- preferential treatment　优惠待遇
- preferred shares (stocks)　优先股
- prejudice to the case　對案情不利
- prejudicial　有成见的,有损害的,不利的,有偏见的
- premeditate　預謀
- premeditated murder　预谋杀人,谋杀
- premises　房地产,房屋(及其附属建筑、土地等)
- prepaid expense　預付費用
- prepayment　預付項目
- preponderance of the evidence　證據的優勢
- prerequisite　先決條件
- prerogative of mercy　赦免权,特赦权
- prescription drugs　處方葯
- present value　現值
- presentation　报告
- presentment agency　檢控代表
- press charges　正式控告

- press 新闻界,新闻,出版,印刷,通讯社
- presumption 推定,推断,假定,推测
- presumption of death 死亡推定
- presumption of fact 事实的推定
- presumption of innocence 無罪推定、無罪假設
- presumption of law 法律上的推定
- presumption of life 生存推定,生命的推定
- presumption of marriage 婚姻的推定
- presumptive evidence 推定证据
- pre-trial conference 审前会议
- pretrial detention 审前拘留
- pretrial discovery 審前互通資料
- pretrial motions 預審動議
- pretrial release 審前暫釋
- pretrial services agency 預審服務機構
- prevailing practice 现行慣例
- prevention of corruption act 防止贪污法令
- preventive detention 防范性拘留,预防性监禁
- preventive maintenance 預防性維修
- previous conviction 案底,前科,过去犯罪记录

- previous offence 前犯,舊犯
- price control 物價控制
- price discrimination 差別定價
- price fixing 價格壟斷
- price index 物價指數
- price leader 價格領袖,誘買價格
- price 價格
- pricing 價格制定
- primary demand 基本需要
- primary market 第一市場,初級市場,基本市場
- primary need 基本需要
- primary product 原產品,初級產品
- primary production 初級生產,第一級生產
- prime cost 主要成本
- prime entry 原始分錄
- prime rate 優惠利率,最優惠利率
- principal 本金,委託人,主事人,當事人
- principal tenant 包租人,二房東
- principle 原理,原則
- principle of contribution 風險分擔原則,攤賠原則

- principle of equality 平等原則
- principle of indemnity 補償原則, 賠償原則
- principle of subrogation 權利代位原則
- prior convictions 前科
- prior year adjustment 前期損益調整
- prison 監獄
- prison clothes 球衣
- prison guard 獄警、管教
- prison sentence 判处监禁
- prisoner 囚犯, 拘留犯, 犯人, 刑事被告, 俘虏
- prisoner under sentence of death 死囚, 死刑犯
- privacy 隱私權
- private law 私法
- private ledger 機密分類帳
- private limited company 私人有限公司
- private property 私有财产
- private treaty 私人合約
- privileged information 秘密資料
- privy council 英国枢密院
- pro forma 暫編的, 預編的

- pro forma balance sheet　暫編資產負債表
- pro forma invoice　臨時發票
- pro forma statement　暫編報表
- pro rata　比例分配
- probable cause　頗能成立的原因
- probate　遗嘱验证,遗嘱认证,遗嘱检验
- probate of codicil　遗嘱附录验证／认证(书)
- probation　缓刑监视,缓刑,检验,验证,鉴定,见习
- probation of will　遗嘱验证,遗嘱检验,遗嘱认证
- probation officer　緩刑犯的官員、緩刑官
- probation order　缓刑令
- probation period　試用期,見習期
- probation revocation　撤消緩刑
- probation termination　終止緩刑
- probation violation　違反緩刑規則
- probationer　受缓刑监视者,试用人员,见习人员
- probative　提供证明的,提供证据的,证明的,鉴定的
- problem　问题,难题
- problem child　问题儿童,难管教的儿童
- problem recognition　問題認知

- problem solving　解決問題
- problem-oriented　問題取向,問題導向
- procedural law　程序法
- procedural matter(s)　程序事項
- procedural　程序上的,
- procedure(s)　程序,手续,办法
- proceeding　程序,进程,进行,行动
- proceedings in rem　对物诉讼,实产诉讼
- proceeds　收入
- process departmentalization　程序分部
- procuration of women　介绍妇女卖淫
- procurement　採購
- producer goods　資本物品,生產者物品
- producer service　工商業支援
- product　產品
- product adaptation　產品適應
- product assortment　產品組合,產品配搭
- product attribute　產品屬性
- product catalogue　產品種類,產品目錄
- product departmentalization　產品分部

- product development　產品發展
- product differentiation　產品差異化
- product diversification　產品多樣化,產品多元化
- product image　產品形象,產品印象
- product life cycle　產品生命循環,產品生命週期
- product line　產品線,產品種類
- product mix　產品組合
- product portfolio　產品組合
- product positioning　產品定位
- product specification　產品規格
- product strategy　產品策略
- production budget　生產預算
- production capacity　生產能力
- production control　生產控制
- production cost　生產成本
- production management　生產管理
- production overhead　生產間接成本
- production planning　生產計畫
- production schedule　生產預算及計畫,生產計畫
- production　生產

- production oriented　生產取向,生產導向
- productivity　生產力
- professional accountant　專業會計師
- professional competence　專業勝任能力
- professional ethics　專業道德,專業操守
- professional independence　專業獨立
- professional misconduct　不正当的专业行为
- professional organization　專業組織
- proffer　認罪條件
- profit and loss appropriation account 損益分配帳
- profit and loss transfer agreement　損益转让协议
- profit margin　利潤率,利潤幅度
- profit motive　課利動機,盈利動機
- profit planning　盈利計畫
- profit reflection　反映利潤
- profit sharing　分紅,利潤分享,利潤分攤
- profit　利润、收益
- profitability　盈利能力,盈利率
- prohibit　禁止,阻止,妨碍,取缔
- prohibition order　禁止令,禁制令

- prohibition 禁止,禁令,不准许,阻止
- promissory note 借據,期票
- promoting gambling 助長賭博
- promoting prostitution 助長賣淫
- promotion 借升,升職,推廣,促進,拓銷
- promotion effortt 推廣效力
- promotion mix 推廣組合
- promotional allowance 促銷折讓,推銷津貼
- promotional pricing 促銷定價法
- prompt cash 當場付款,即時付款,日內付款
- proof of will 遺嘱证明,遺嘱认证
- proof 证据,凭据,证明,校稿
- property 财产,地产,物(权),财产权,所有权
- proposal form 保險申請表,動議表格
- proposed dividend 據派股息
- proprietary interest 資本權益,東主權益
- proprietor 所有人,业主,拥有人
- proprietorship 所有权,业主权
- pros and cons 正与反,赞成者和反对者
- prosecution witness 控方证人

- prosecution 检察当局,控告,提控,起诉,检举
- prosecutor 主控官,检察司,公诉人,原告,检举人
- prospectus 招股章程,招股書
- prostitute 娼妓,妓女,卖身者,卖淫者
- prostitution 卖淫,操淫业,娼妓业
- protection of minorities 保障少数的权益
- protection racket 勒索保護費的組織
- protectionism 保護主義
- protectionist measure 貿易保護措施
- protectionist policy 保護主義政策
- protective custody 保護性拘留、監護
- protective order 保護令
- protest a bill 票據拒付通知
- protest fee 拒付通知費
- provident fund scheme 公積金計畫
- provision 準備
- provision for bad debts 呆帳準備
- provision for depreciation 折舊準備
- provision for discounts allowed 銷貨折扣準備
- provision for unrealised profit 未實現利潤準備

- provision of professional　提供專業人士
- provisional certificate　临时证书,临时执照
- provisional order　临时令
- provocation　刺激,挑拨,激愤
- proximate cause　近因
- prudence　穩健保守,審慎
- prudence principle　谨慎性原则
- psychological need　心理需要
- psychotoxic chemicals　引起精神病的化學品
- public accountant, auditor　审计师、会计师
- public company　上市公司
- public corporation　公營公司
- public defender　公設辯護人/律師
- public domain　公有領域/產業/土地
- public enterprise　公營企業
- public law　公法
- public lewdness　當眾猥褻
- public monies　公款
- public property　公有物,公有财产,公产
- public relations　公共關係

- public utilities　公共事業,公用事業
- publicity　宣傳
- published accounts　公開發表的報表
- punishment　刑罚,处罚,罚
- punitive damages　惩罚性的损害赔偿费,
- punitive　惩罚性的,刑罚的,给予惩处的
- purchase　購貨
- purchase contract　購貨契約
- purchased goodwill　購買商譽
- purchases journal　購貨簿
- purchases ledger　應付帳款分類帳
- purchases returns book　購貨退回簿
- purchases returns　購貨退回
- purchasing management　採購管理
- purchasing power　購買力
- pure profit　純盈利
- pure risk　純風險
- pursuit　追捕
- put option　认沽期权

# Q

- qualification 資格
- qualified title 有条件的产权,受限制的房地产权
- quality certificate 品质证明书
- quality circle 品質控制圈,品質圈,品管圈
- quality control circle 品質控制圈,品質圈
- qualm 疑慮
- quantifiability 可數量性
- quantity 數目、數量
- quantity discount 數量折扣,大批量折扣
- quantum 定量,总量
- quantum meruit 按照工作服务计酬,按劳计酬
- quantum of damages 损害赔偿金数额
- quarantine 檢疫隔離
- quasi 宛如
- quasi partner 準合夥人
- quasi reorganisation 準改組,帳面改組

- quasi-contract　准契约,准合同
- quasi-judicial　准司法的,具有部分司法权的
- quasi-liquidation　准清盘,准清算
- question　讯问,提问,发问,询问,问题
- question of law　法律问题
- question of liability　赔偿责任的问题
- question of order　程序问题
- questionable　有问题的,不可靠的,可疑的
- questionable conduct　可疑的行为
- questionable person　可疑的人
- questionable statement　不可靠的陈述
- quick asset　速動資產
- quick court　短期法庭
- quick liability　速動負債
- quick ratio　速動比率
- quid pro quo　交換條件、抵償物
- quiet possession　不受幹擾享用權
- quorum　法定人數
- quota　定額,配額,限額
- quotation　報價,報價單

- quoted company　上市公司
- quoted market price　開列的市價
- quoted securities investment　有價證券投資

# R

- racism 種族主義
- racketeering 敲詐勒索
- racketeering enterprise 敲詐勒索集團
- radar detector 雷達探測器
- radar speed gun 雷達速度測試器
- radical 激進、極端
- rail transport 鐵路運輸
- railroad crossing 鐵路公路交叉道口
- random sampling 隨機抽樣
- ransack 洗劫、徹底搜查
- ransom 贖金
- rape 強姦
- rate 率
- rate of exchange 匯兌率
- rate of return 報酬率,收益率,盈利率,回報率
- rate of stockturn 存貨周轉率

- rate of turnover 周轉率
- to ratify 批准、認可
- ratio 比率
- ratio analysis 比率分析
- raw data 原始數據
- raw material 原料
- to read law 攻讀法律
- real 不动产的,真正的,现实的,实在,实际
- real account 實帳戶
- real cost 實際成本
- real estate 不动产,房地产
- real price 實際價格
- real property/real state 不動產、房地產
- real value 實際價值
- real wage 實際工資
- realisable income 可實現收益
- realisable value 可變現值
- realisation account 變現帳戶,變產帳戶
- realisation convention 收入實現原則
- realisation expense 變現費用,變產費用

- to realise 變現
- realised appreciation 已實現漲價
- realised profit 已實現利潤
- realised revenue 已實現收益
- realization of property 变卖财产
- realty 不動產
- rearrest notification 重新逮捕通知
- reasonable 合理的
- reasonable care 合理的關注
- reasonable cause 合理原因
- reasonable doubt 合理的懷疑
- reasonable excuse 合理解释,合理原因
- reasonable force 合理武力
- rebate 回扣,回傭,退稅
- rebuttable presumption 可辩驳的假定
- rebuttal 反駁
- recall a witness 召回證人
- recapitalisation 調整資本,資本重組,資本重定
- receipt 收据
- receivables 应收款项

- receiver　接管人,收件人
- receivership　接管人的职务／职位
- receivership account　財產接管會計,破產清算會計
- receiving stolen property　收受贓物
- recess　休息
- recession　衰退
- recidivist　慣犯、累犯
- reckless assault　魯莽侵犯
- reckless burning　魯莽用火
- reckless driving　魯莽駕駛
- reckless endangerment　任意危害罪
- recognizance　保證（到庭）
- reconciliation　和解,調解,調停
- reconciliation statement　調節表
- reconstruction　重建
- record　記錄
- recorded delivery　記錄派遞
- to recourse　追索权,偿还请求,求偿权
- recover　取得,追讨,讨回,收回,取回,重新获得
- recover damage　取得赔偿,补偿损失

- recoverable amount　可收回金額
- recoverable　可追回的,可予追討,可收回的
- recovery　收回,追索,取得
- recreational vehicles　大型旅行車
- recross　再次盤問
- recruitment　招募,招聘,聘任
- recurrent expenditure　經常開支
- to recuse　迴避
- recycling　再循環
- redeem　贖回,償清,償还
- redeem a mortgage　贖回抵押品
- redeemable preference share　可贖回優先股
- redemption　贖回,償还,还清,(证券)变卖成现款
- redirect　再次直接詢問
- redress　补偿,补救,矫正,纠正,平反
- redundancy　裁員，多餘,冗餘
- to reexamine　再审问,再审查
- re-export　轉口,轉口貨
- reference　援引
- reference check　背景調查

- referent power　認同權力
- referral　轉介,推薦,介紹
- refugee　難民
- refund　归还、退还
- register of death　死亡登記
- registered bond　記名債券
- registered capital　註冊資本,註冊股本,法定股本
- registered trademark　註冊商標
- Registrar General's Department　註冊總署
- Registrar of Companies　公司註冊官
- registration (auto)（汽車）上牌/登記
- registration of companies　公司註冊
- regulation　准則,規定
- regulator　規管機構,監管機構
- regulatory body　監管機構
- regulatory framework of accounting　會計監管架構
- rehabilitation　改造
- rehabilitative measures　改造措施
- reimbursement　補償,報銷
- reinforcement/reinforce　強化物,強化

- reinstated 恢復
- reinsurance 再保險,分保
- relating to other periods 其他期間的
- relation(s) 亲属,家属
- release pending trail 得釋在外待審
- release 釋放
- relevance 相關性,切題性
- relevant cost 相關成本
- relevant range 相關範圍
- relevant revenue 相關收入
- reliability 可靠性,信度,可靠程度
- reliable disclosure 披露可靠資料
- remains (body) 殘骸、遺骸
- remand 還押
- to remand 發回重審
- remedy 補救
- reminder advertising 提醒性廣告
- remittance 匯款
- remittance advice note 匯款通知書
- remittance slip 匯款付單

- remote cause　远因,间接原因
- remote damages　间接损害,间接损失
- removal hearing　移送聆訊
- remuneration　薪酬,酬勞
- rendu　賣方負責運費之報價
- renegotiation　重議價
- renewal　更新,換新
- rent　租金
- rental contract　租赁合同
- rental income　租赁收入
- renunciation　弃权声明书
- reorder level/re-order level　再定貨水平
- reorder point/re-order point　再訂貨點,再訂購點
- reorganization　改組,改編,重新編訂
- repairs and maintenance　修理及保養維修
- reparations　賠償、賠款
- repayment　归还(借款)、偿还
- repeat offender　慣犯
- repeat offense　多次罪行
- replacement, substitute　替代、取代

- replacement cost　重置成本
- replacement depreciation method　重置成本折舊法
- replacement requirement　替換要求
- replacement transfer　位置替代
- reply　回答,答复
- reports　报告
- repossession　收回已出售之貨品
- represent a client　代表客戶
- represent to the court　向法官陳述
- representative　代表,代理人
- reputation　聲譽,信譽
- requisition　申請單,請求單
- res　物,物体,事件
- res integra　专决定的要点、问题
- res ipsa loquitur　事情不言自明,事情不证自明
- res judicata　已判决事件,已判决的事项
- resale　轉賣
- reseller　分銷商
- reserve　準備,儲備,公積金
- reserve currency　储备货币

- reserve for amortisation 攤銷準備
- reserve for bad debts 呆帳準備
- reserve for contingency 應急準備
- reserve for depletion 耗竭準備
- reserve for depreciation 折舊準備
- reserve fund 準備金,儲備基金
- residence 住所、私宅
- resident 居民,居住者
- residential treatment 住院治療
- residual cost 剩餘成本
- residual property 剩余财产,余产
- residual value 剩餘價值,殘值
- resisting arrest 拒捕
- resolution 决定、决议
- resource 資源
- respondent 答辩人
- responsibility 責任
- rest a case 案件證據已全部提出
- restitution and reparation 賠償和補償
- restitution 归还,偿还

- restraining order 抑制令,制止令
- restraint 控制、抑制、制止,约束,限制
- restraint of marriage 限制婚姻
- restricted licence bank 有限制持牌銀行
- restriction order 限制令
- restructuring 重整、改建、改组
- result from ordinary operations 正常营业损益
- result management 結果管理法,成效管理
- retain or replace equipment 保留或轉換機器
- retail banking 零售性銀行業務
- retail cooperative society 零售合作社
- retail price 零售價
- retail theft 盜竊零售商品
- retail trade 零售業,零售貿易
- retailer 零售商
- retained earnings 營業盈餘,留存盈餘,保留盈餘
- retained profit 留存利潤
- retention of title 所有权之保留
- retired bill 已贖回票據
- retired partner 已退休之合夥人

- retirement 退休,退股,贖回,報廢
- retirement benefits 退休金、养老金
- retirement protection 退休保障
- retirement scheme 退休金計畫
- retract 撤回
- retribution 懲罰
- retroactive 有追溯效力的
- retroactive basis 追溯基礎
- retrospective 追溯
- return a verdict 作出判決
- return of sales 销售回报率
- return on investment 投資報酬率,投資回報率
- returns inward 銷貨退回
- returns outward book 購貨退出簿
- returns outward 購貨退出
- revaluation reserve 重估準備,估值準備
- revaluation 重估
- revenue 收益,收入,營業收入
- revenue expenditure 收益支出,營業支出
- revenue receipt 營業收入,已收收入

- revenue reserve 留存利润
- revenue statement 收益表
- reversal (判决等的)推翻,撤销,废弃,反转
- reversal of judgment 撤销原判,推翻原判
- reversing entry 還原分錄,回轉分錄
- revocable letter of credit 可撤銷信用證
- revocation 撤消
- revoke 撤銷、吊銷、取消
- revolt 叛變、造反
- revolver 左輪槍
- revolving credit 輪迴式賒帳,輪迴式信貸
- rifle 來復槍
- right 權利
- right of monopoly 专有权,专卖权
- right of property 财产权
- right of recourse 追償權,求償權,请求返还权
- right of recovery 追償權,请求归还权
- right of reply 答辩权
- right of search 搜查权
- right of self-defence 自卫权

- right of succession　继承权
- right(s) of claim　索偿权,索赔权
- right-of-way　先行權、通行權
- rights issue　股權發行,供股
- risk assessment　风险评估
- risk assumption　風險承擔
- risk avoidance　風險迴避
- risk capital　風險資本
- risk diversification　風險分散
- risk hierarchy　風險等級
- risk identification　風險界定
- risk level　風險水平
- risk management　風險管理
- risk measurement　風險量度
- risk of flight　潛逃危機
- risk of loss　损失之虞,损失的风险
- risk pooling　風險分擔,風險匯合,風險匯聚
- risk reduction　風險減少
- risk spreading　風險攤分
- risk transfer　風險轉移

- robbery　抢劫(罪)
- robbery, armed　持械搶劫
- round lot　成批,股票成交單位,股票買賣單位
- rule(s)　裁决,裁定,章程,条例,规则,法规
- rule of law　法治
- rule of practice　诉讼程序法规
- rule of survivorship　生存者取得权的原则
- rule(s) of evidence　证据法规
- rule(s) of law　法律规则,法律原则,法治
- rule(s) of order　会议规则
- rule(s) of practice　诉讼程序法规
- rule(s) of procedure　议事规则
- rules of court　法院规则
- rules of evidence　證據法規則
- ruling　裁决,裁定,规定
- running cost　營運成本
- running down case　撞车事件损害赔偿诉案

# S

- sabotage 蓄意破壞、怠工
- sacrilege 瀆聖、冒瀆
- sadism 虐待狂
- safe 安全的,可靠的,可信賴的
- safe conduct 通過許可(证),安全通行(证),护送
- safe deposit box 保管箱
- safe keeping 妥善保管,妥善保护
- safety need 安全需要,安全感需要
- safety regulation 安全規則
- safety stock 安全存貨
- salary 薪水,工资
- sale 銷貨
- sales allowance 銷貨折讓
- sales book 銷貨簿
- sales budget 銷售預算,銷貨預算
- sales day book 銷貨日記簿

- sales deductions    销售损失
- sales discount    銷貨折扣
- sales invoice    銷貨發票
- sales journal    銷貨簿
- sales ledger    應收帳款分類帳
- sales promotion    促銷,銷售推廣,銷售促進
- sales quota    目標銷售額,銷售配額
- sales oriented    銷售導向,銷售取向
- salvage value    殘值
- sampling    抽樣
- sanction    认可,批准,核准,许可,制裁,惩罚
- to satisfy    偿还,清偿,履行,满足
- satisfy debt    还清债务
- savings account    儲蓄存款帳戶,儲蓄帳戶
- savings bank    储蓄银行
- scene of crime    作案現場
- schedule, attachment    附件、附表
- scheduling    日程安排
- scientific management    科學管理
- scontinued operatives    终止经营业务

- scope 范围
- scrap dividend 期票股利,股利票
- scrap issue 紅股發行,期票股利發行
- scrap value 殘值
- screening 甄別,甄選
- scrip dividend 期票股利,票據股利,股利票
- sea transport 水上運輸
- seal the record 封案
- search 搜查
- to search 搜查,调查,检查
- search and seizure 搜查与充公
- search warrant 搜查令
- search without warrant 擅自进行搜查
- seasonal fluctuation 季節性波動
- seasonal variation 季節性變動
- second degree murder 二級謀殺
- secondary data 次級資料,二手數據
- secondary market 第二市場,次級市場,交易市場
- secondary production 第二級生產,次級生產
- secret agent 特務、特工

- secret matters　秘密事件
- secret partner　秘密合夥人,隱名合夥人
- secret reserve　秘密準備
- Secret Service　特勤部
- sectional ledger　分組分類帳
- secured　有抵押
- secured debenture　有抵押債券
- secured loan　有擔保貸款,有抵押放款
- security　安全,安稳,保证,担保,抵押,治安
- security fraud　證券欺詐
- security need　安全感需要,安全需要
- security, guarantee　抵押，担保
- sedition　煽動叛亂
- seditious intention　煽动意图,煽动暴乱意图
- seditious libel　煽动性诽谤
- seduction　引诱,勾引,诱拐,诱惑
- seizable offence　可被拘捕的罪行
- seizure　依法占有,没收,充公,扣押,查封
- self defense　自衛，正當防衛
- self determination　自决

- self incrimination　自証其罪、自我牽連
- self actualisation need　自我實現需要
- self appraisal　自我評核
- self balancing　自行平衡
- self insurance　自保,自辦保險
- self service　自助
- self-sufficient　自給自足
- sell or process further　出售或加工
- semi-automatic gun　半自動槍械
- semi-finished product　半製成品
- semi-manufactured product　半製成品
- semi-variable cost　半變動成本
- seniority　年資,工齡
- sense of belonging　歸屬感
- sense of responsibility　責任感
- separate financial statements　个別财务报表
- separation agreement　分居協議
- separation　分居
- sequester a jury　隔離陪審團
- serial bond　分批還本債券,分期還本債券

- serve a subpoena 送達傳票
- serve papers on a party 送交文件給某方
- service 服務
- service strategy 服務策略
- set bail 定保釋金額
- set up cost 準備成本,裝置成本
- settlement judge 调解法官
- sever case 將案件分離
- severance 断绝,割断
- sex offense 性犯罪
- sexual abuse 性虐待
- sexual assault 性侵犯
- sexual desire 性欲
- sexual intercourse 性交
- sexual misconduct 不軌的性行為
- sexual offence 性罪行
- sexual predator 性侵犯者
- sham 假的,虛假的,假裝,佯作,欺骗,假冒
- sham defence 假辩护,虚伪的答辨
- sham plea 虚伪的答辨

- to share 股票
- share capital 股本
- share premium 股本溢價
- share subscription 股本認購,股票認購
- shareholder 股東
- sheriff （縣）警長
- shift duty 輪班工作
- shift system 輪班制度,輪班工作
- shift work 輪班工作
- shipping law 海运法
- shoplifting 在商店行竊的行為
- shopping goods 選購品,選購貨品
- short position 賣空,淡倉合約,賣出的期貨合約
- short selling 賣空,拋空
- short term 短期
- short term capital 短期資本,短期資金
- short term financing 短期籌資
- short term liability 短期負債
- short term loan 短期貸款
- shotgun 散彈槍、獵槍

- sight draft　即期票據,即期匯票
- signature　签名,署名,签署
- silent partner　靜默合夥人,隱名合夥人
- silver currency　银币
- similar land rights　准地产权益
- simultaneous interpretation　同聲傳譯
- sine die　无限期,不定期
- sine qua non　必要的条件,必具的资格
- single-entry bookkeeping　單式簿記
- sinking fund bond　償債基金債券
- sinking fund depreciation method　償債基金折舊法
- sinking fund　償債基金
- skid row　貧民區街道、沒落地段
- skimming pricing　爭取更多利潤的訂價策略
- slander　(口头的)诽谤,造谣,中伤,诋毁
- slander of goods　诽谤货物(品质),商品诽谤
- slavery　奴隸制
- slip and fall　滑倒
- slowdown　怠工,放慢
- smuggling　走私

- social accounting  社會會計
- social cost  社會成本,公損,社會代價
- social insurance contributions  社会保险费
- social need  社會需要,社群需要
- social responsibility  社會責任
- social security  社会保险
- social status  社會地位
- socialism  社會主義
- socialist market economy  社會主義市場經濟體系
- sole agent  總代理,獨家代理商
- sole discretion  全权处理,单独酌处权
- sole proprietor  獨資經營者，獨資企業
- sole proprietor  唯一业主,独资人
- sole proprietorship  獨資經營,獨資企業
- sole trader  全東,東主，獨資經營
- solemnize  举行仪式,举行典礼
- solicitation  教唆、拉客
- solicitor  法務官
- solicitor-general  副总检察长
- to solve a case  破案

- solvency　償付能力,清償能力
- source of financing　融資方式
- span of control　控制幅度,管理寬度
- span of management　管理寬度
- spare parts　备件
- special agent　特務、特工
- special court　特別法庭,专理法庭
- special damages　特別损害赔偿(金)
- special economic zone　經濟特區
- special verdict　特別裁决
- specialisation　專門化,專業化,專科化,專門知識
- specialised staff　專業幕僚，專業人員
- specialty goods　特殊品,特殊貨品
- specialty store　特殊店,特殊店舖
- specialty wholesaler　專門批發商
- specific performance　強制履行令,特定履行令
- specification　規格
- speculation　投機
- speculative motive　投機動機
- speculative risk　投機風險

- speculator 投機者
- speedball [mix of cocaine & heroin] 強效興奮劑
- speedy trial 快速審理
- split sentence 分罰的判刑
- split-off point 分離點
- spot cash 付現
- spot deal 即時交易,即時買賣
- spot delivery 即時交收
- spot market 現貨市場
- spot price 現貨價格
- spreadsheet 試算表
- squatter 擅自居住、
- staff efficiency 員工工作效率
- staff function 員工功能,員工職能
- staff organisation 員工組織
- staffing function 人力功能
- staffing 員工編制
- stagnation 停滯
- stakeholder 持分者
- stale cheque 過期支票

- stalking 反復騷擾和威脅，威脅性的跟蹤
- stamp duty 印花稅
- stamp office 印花稅局
- stand-alone project 獨立項目
- standard cost 標準成本
- standard deviation 標準偏差
- standard of living 生活水平
- standard price 标准单价
- standard tax rate 標準稅率
- standardization 標準化
- standards 標準
- standing order 定期支付指示，經常訂單
- standing rule(s) 常行規則,办事規則
- starboard 右边,右舷
- start up capital 創業資金
- state land 国有土地,国家土地
- state of emergency 緊急狀態
- state of intoxication 醉酒狀態
- state of property 国有财产,国家财产
- state 国家,州,狀态,情况

- stated value  設定價值
- statement in answer to the charge  答辯控罪陈述书
- statement of account  會計帳目，結單
- statement of affairs  清理式資產負債表
- statement of bank account  银行对帐单
- statement of changes in  股东权益变动表
- statement of defence  答辩陈述,被告的抗辩声明
- statement of fact  案情,事实陈述
- statement of offence  罪行陈述书,罪行摘要
- statement  供述,陈述,声明,报表
- static budget  靜態預算,固定預算
- status inquiry agency  狀況諮詢機構
- status offender  未到法定年齡的犯事者
- status offense  未到法定年齡的犯事
- status quo  現狀
- statute law  成文法,制定法
- statute of frauds  防止欺骗法令,禁止诈欺法
- statute of limitation  時效法規
- statute  法令,成法规,成文法律,制定法
- statutory  法定的,法令的,依照法令的

- statutory declaration 法定宣誓(书)
- statutory information 法定资料
- statutory law 成文法、制定法
- statutory offence 法定罪行
- statutory order 法令
- statutory provision 法定条文, 法律规定
- statutory rape 法定强奸
- statutory reserve 法定留存、公积金
- statutory rule(s) and order(s) 制定法规和命令
- statutory supervision 法定监视
- stay 暂缓
- stay a warrant 中止刑事手令
- stay of execution 延期执行, 中止执行
- stay of proceedings 中止诉讼程序
- step cost 梯級成本
- stewardship concept 管理責任概念
- stickup 搶劫
- stipulation 規定、協議
- stipulation of settlement 協議, 協議書
- stock 存貨, 證券, 股票

- stock broker    證券經紀,股票經紀
- stock control    存貨控制,存貨管理,存貨管制
- stock exchange    證券交易所,股票交易所
- stock in hand    商品存貨
- stock level    存貨水平
- stock market    證券市場,股票市場
- stock option    認股特權,認股權
- stock reserve    存貨準備
- stock split    拆股
- stock take    盘点、盘存
- stock turnover    存貨周轉,存貨周轉率
- stock valuation    存貨計價,存貨估值
- stockholder    股東
- stockholders' meeting    股东大会
- stockjobber    證券批銷經紀
- stock-out cost    缺貨成本
- stolen property    贓物
- stop and frisk    停住搜身
- stop and search power    截查权
- straight-line depreciation method    直線折舊法

- strangulation 勒死、絞死
- strategic planning 策略規畫
- stratified sampling 分層抽樣
- strict confidence 绝对保密
- strict liability 後果上的責任
- strike from the record 從紀錄中刪除
- strike 罷工
- structural unemployment 結構性失業
- structured deposit 結構性存款
- structured interview 結構性面談
- stupefying drugs 迷幻药
- sub judice 审理中的,尚未判决的,在法庭中
- subcontract 转包合同,分包合同
- subcontracting 轉契承包,轉包,分包合約
- sub-group (of companies) 集团分公司
- subject to endorsement 背书后始生效
- subject to prosecution 可被公訴
- sublease 转租、转租权
- sublet 分租,转租
- submission 陈词,在法庭陈述辩词,递呈,提交

- submit evidence 提出證據
- subordinate 部屬,下屬
- subordinate courts 初级法院
- suborn perjury 唆使提供僞證
- subpoena duces tecum 携带证件出庭的传票
- subrogation 權利代位,債權移轉
- subscribed capital 认缴股本
- subscription 會費,訂購費,訂購,認購
- subsequent date 后期
- subsidiary 子公司
- subsidiary account 補助分類帳戶,明細分類帳戶
- subsidiary company 附屬公司,子公司
- subsidy 补贴、津贴
- substance 实质,本质,实体,物质,内容,资产
- substance abuse prevention 防止濫用藥物的措施
- substance abuse 濫用藥物
- substance over form 實質重於形式
- substantial 物质的,实质的,实体的,真实的
- substantial argument 重要的论证
- substantial shareholder 大股東,主要股東

- substantive law　實體法、主法
- substituted petitioner　替代上诉人
- subtenancy　转租,转借
- subtenant　转租人
- succession of property　遗产继承,财产继承
- succession　继承,继承权,继承顺序
- successor　继承人,继任者,接班人,后继人
- to sue　起訴、打官司
- suicide verdict　自杀裁决
- summary conviction　即决裁定,即席裁决
- summary dismissal　即决撤职,即决驳回
- summary judgment　即决審判
- summary punishment　即决处罚
- summons　传票,传唤
- sum-of-the-years-digits method　年數總和法
- sundry expense　雜費
- super profit　超越利潤
- superintendent　總管,主管
- superior goods　優等物品
- superior　上司,上級

- supervision 監督
- supervisor 管理人員,監督,主管
- supervisory board 監事会
- supplement 补遗,增补,补编,附件,补件
- supplementary rule(s) 附則
- supplier 供應者
- suppress evidence 壓制證據
- supreme court 最高法院
- surcharge 附加費
- surety bond 保證債券
- surface mail 平郵
- surplus 盈餘
- surrender value 退還金額,退保金額
- surrogate 代理者,替代人
- surveillance 監視
- survivorship 生存者取得权,生还,生存
- susceptible 易受影響的
- suspect 疑犯 犯罪嫌疑人
- suspected of being guilty 有犯罪嫌疑
- suspend a driving licence 吊销驾车执照

- suspend judgment　缓期宣判
- suspend sentence　缓期处刑
- suspend　中止,暂停,悬而不决
- suspended judgment　暫緩判決
- suspended license　暫時吊銷執照
- suspended sentence　緩刑 緩刑
- suspense account　暫記帳戶
- suspicion　嫌疑,怀疑
- to sustain 维持,证实,认可,蒙受
- sustainability　可持续性
- sustainable　可持續的
- to swear to tell the truth　發誓說實話
- swindle　行骗,欺诈,诈骗,欺骗,骗术
- swindler　骗子,诈骗者
- swipe credit card　刷信用卡
- sworn testimony　宣誓作證
- syndicate　財團,集團,企業組合
- syndicated loan　組合貸款,集團貸款,銀團貸款
- synergetic effect　協同效應
- system　制度,体制,体系,系统

- system analysis 系統分析
- system analyst 系統分析員
- system design 系統設計
- system of recourse 求償制度

# T

- tacit approval　默許
- tacit understanding　默契
- tactical planning　戰術規畫,戰術計畫,具體計畫
- to take issue　提出異議
- to take the stand　到證人席作證、出庭作證
- takeover　收購, 接管,接收
- takeover bid　收購行動,收購競爭
- taking into custody　拘押
- takings　營業額
- to tampered with　窜改过
- tampering with a consumer product　對消費品的干預
- tampering with a witness　干擾證人
- tampering with evidence　損壞證據
- tampering with jury　干預陪審團
- tangible asset　有形資產
- tangible product　有形產品

- tare weight　皮重,容器重量
- target market　目標市場
- target profit　目標利潤
- tariff　關稅
- tax　稅,稅款,稅捐
- tax advantage　有利稅率
- tax adviser　稅務顧問
- tax allowance　免稅額
- tax audit　稅務審計
- tax avoidance　避稅
- tax balance sheet　稅務資產負債平衡表
- tax bureau　財政局、稅務局
- tax collection office　稅務徵收處
- tax declaration　納稅申報表
- tax deduction　減稅
- tax demand　徵稅單、徵稅通知書
- tax estimation　稅款估計
- tax evasion　逃稅
- tax exemption　免稅
- tax expense　稅務費用

- tax fraud 稅務行騙
- tax free 免稅
- tax law 稅法
- tax liability 纳税义务
- tax privileged 税收优惠
- tax rate 稅率
- tax regime 稅制
- tax return 稅表、報稅單
- tax shelter 合法避稅手段
- taxation 课税、税金
- technical skill 技術技能
- technical violation 技術上違規
- technological change 技術轉變
- technology-intensive 技術密集型
- telecommunication 電信,電訊
- telecommunications fraud 電信行騙
- telephone fraud 電話行騙
- telex 專用電報
- temporary insanity 暫時性精神錯
- temporary order of protection 暫時保護令

- temporary restraining order 暂时禁令 暫時禁令
- tenancy 出租
- tenancy at will 可任意取消的租赁
- tenant 承租人,租户,房客
- tenant for life 终身租户,终身租借人
- tenant for years 以若干年为期的土地租借人
- tenants in common 合有人,分权共有人
- tender 投标
- tenement 地产,保有物,享有物,住宅,共同住宅
- tenor (gist) 要旨、大意
- tentative 暂定的 暫定的
- tenure 占有,占有期,占有条件,占有权,任期
- term 期限,期间,地产租用期,偿债期
- term loan 定期放款,定期借款
- term of payment 清偿期
- term of validity 有效期
- terminal value 终值
- termination of tenancy 租赁期满
- termination 结束,终止,末端
- terms 条件,条款,术语

- terms of agreement  合约的条件
- terms of loan  货款的条件
- terms of payment  付款的条件
- terms of reference  職權範圍
- terms of service  服務條件
- terms of settlement  和解條件
- terms of trade  貿易價格比率,貿易比率
- territorial departmentalisation  區域分部
- terrorism  恐怖主義
- terrorist  恐怖分子
- tertiary production  第三級生產
- test market  測試市場
- test marketing  試銷
- testamentary gift  遺贈
- testate  立有遺囑的
- testator  遺囑人,立有遺囑者
- testatrix  女遺囑人
- testificandum  立证
- testification  证据,证明,作证,立证,证言
- to testify  作證

- testimony 证言,证词,口供,证据
- testimony of witness 证人供证
- theft 盜竊
- time deposit 定期存款
- time draft 期付匯票,定期匯票
- time for adjudication 宣判日期
- time immemorial 法律上无法追溯的年代
- time limit 期限,限期
- time of payment 付款期
- time off for good behavior 因表現良好而減刑
- time policy 時限保單,定期保險單
- time rate 計時工資,計時收費率
- time served 已服刑期
- time study 時間研究
- time utility 時間效用
- time value of money 金錢的時間值
- timeliness 及時性
- title deed 房地契,地契,所有权契據,产权契据
- title insurance 產權保險
- title 所有权,所有权凭证,契据,产权,房地契

- tobacco product warning 煙草產品警告
- top management 上層管理,高層管理人員
- top manager 高層管理人員
- tort (民事的)侵权行为
- tortfeasor 侵权者,侵权行为人
- tortious 侵权的
- torture 拷问,拷打,严刑,折磨,痛苦,虐待,歪曲
- total account 總帳戶
- total assets turnover 總資產周轉率
- total creditors account 應付帳款分類帳統制帳戶
- total debtors account 應收帳款分類帳統制帳戶
- total incapacity 全无资格,完全无能力
- total loss 全部亏损,全损,完全损失
- total performance 全部清償
- tout 拉生意,招徕顾客
- trace 痕跡
- trade acceptance 商業承兌票據
- trade accounts payablee 应付货款
- trade accounts receivable 应收帐款
- trade association 商會

- trade barrier    貿易障礙,貿易壁壘
- trade credit    貿易賒帳,商業信用
- trade creditor    購貨債權人,購貨客戶
- trade cycle    商業循環,商業週期
- trade debtor    銷貨債務人,銷貨客戶
- trade discount    交易折扣,營業折扣
- trade dispute    勞資糾紛,勞資爭議
- trade mark    商標
- trade mission    貿易團,貿易代表團
- trade names    商品/商號/商業名稱
- trade organization    貿易組織
- trade promotion    貿易促進,商業促進
- trade register    工商登记
- trade restriction    貿易限制
- trade union    工會,職工會
- trade-in value    易新價值,以舊換新價值
- trademark    商標
- trademark counterfeiting    偽造商標
- traders' credit    商人放帳額,同行放帳
- trading account    購銷帳

- trading and profit and loss account　購銷損益帳
- trading capital　營運資金
- trading partner　貿易夥伴
- trading profit　毛利
- trading stock　商品庫存
- traffic　交通,,交易,貿易,吞吐量
- traffic accident　交通事故
- traffic citation　交通罰單
- traffic court　交通法庭
- traffic offence　交通罪行,违反交通条例
- trafficking　非法买卖,非法贩卖
- training　訓練,培訓
- tramp steamer　不定期貨船
- transaction　交易事項
- transcript　紀錄抄本
- transfer of cause　讼案的移审,案件转移
- transfer price　轉移價格
- transition　过渡
- transliteration　音譯
- transparent　透明度

- transportation system　運輸系統
- transportation-in　購貨運費
- transportation-out　銷貨運費
- transposition error　數位調換錯誤
- travelling expense　交通費
- traverse of indictment　否认控诉
- treason　叛国罪,叛逆罪,不忠,背信
- treasury shares　庫存股
- treasury stock (own shares)　庫存股票
- treatment　处理,治疗,待遇
- trend analysis　趨勢分析
- trespass　未经许可进入私人土地,非法侵入,侵犯
- trespasser　侵犯者,侵犯他人土地者,不法侵入者
- trespassing　擅自進入
- trial　审判,审讯,试用
- trial balance　試算表
- trial by jury　由陪审团进行的审讯,陪审审判
- trial court　审讯法庭
- trial on merit　實體審判
- tribunal　审判员席,法官席

- trickster 骗子,欺骗者
- trier of fact 事實的審判者
- triggering event 触发事件
- truancy 曠課、逃學、礦工
- truant officer 調查曠課/礦工的官員
- true and fair view 真確及公正意見
- true bill 大陪審團簽署的起訴書
- true statement 真实供词
- trumped up charge 誣告、無中生有
- trust deed 信託契據
- trust fund 信託基金
- trust receipt 信託收條
- trustee 受託人,信託人
- trusteeship 信托制度,托管制度,信托人的职责
- trustworthiness 可信賴性
- truth 真实,真相,真理
- truthful statement 真實聲明
- turn-around time 運轉時間,周轉期
- turnover 周轉,營業額,銷售量,員工流動

- turpis causa    不道德的约因,不道德代价
- type    类型

# U

- ulterior motives  别有用心的动机,隐秘不明的动机
- ultimatum  最后通牒,哀的美敦书,最后结论
- ultra vires  超越(的),越权(的)
- un alienable right  不容剝奪的權利
- unanimous  (全体)一致的
- unanimous verdict  全體一致的判決
- unauthorized  未经授权的,未经获准的,未经许可的
- unauthorized use of a vehicle  未經授權使用車輛
- unauthorized use of credit card  未經授權使用信用卡
- unavoidable cost  不可避免成本
- unavoidable risk  無法避免之風險
- uncalled capital  末催繳股本
- uncaused  无前因的,无原因的
- uncertainty  无定性,无常
- unclaimed dividend  未領股利
- unconstitutional  違憲

- unconditional leave    无条件批准
- unconditional release/discharge    無條件釋放
- undeclared    未申报的,未经宣布的
- undefended    无辩护的,未防备的
- undefined    未阐明的,未解释的,未下定义的
- undeniable    无可争辩的,不可否认的,不会错的
- under advisement    會考慮周全
- under capitalization    資本過少
- under oath    宣過誓
- under penalty of    處以….的懲罰
- undercast    少計
- undercover officer    密探
- understandability    可理解性
- understanding    理解,谅解,协议,协定
- understatement    少報,少計
- undersubscription    認購不足
- undervaluation    估價過低
- to underwrite    承保、負責保險、負責支付
- underwriter    承保人,保险商,承购人,包销
- underwriting    包銷

- underwriting contract 承保合約
- undifferentiated marketing 無差異營銷
- undischarged 未履行的,(债务)未偿清的,未清理的
- undisputed 无可争辩的,毫无疑问的,无需争论的
- undistributed profit 未分派之盈利,未分派利潤
- undivided 未分割的,不可分割的,完整的
- undue 不正当的,过分的,未到期的,威胁手段
- unearned income 遞延收益,預收收益
- unemployed 失业的
- unemployment rate 失業率
- unencumbered 没有(抵押、债务等）负担,不受妨碍的
- unenforceable 不能强制执行的,不能实行的
- unequivocal 不含糊的,不容置疑的
- unexecuted 未根据条款履行的,未执行的
- unfair 不公平,不正直,不公正
- unfair competitive practice 不公平競爭
- unfair trade practice 不公平貿易手段
- unfit 不胜任的
- unforeseen 预料不到的,不可预知的
- unfortified (论据)不牢靠的

- unidentified 来路不明的
- uniform crime reporting 統一的罪案報告方式
- unilateral 单方面的,一方的
- unilateral contract 单方承担义务的合同,单务合同
- unilateral obligation 单方债务
- unilateral repudiation 单方否认,单方拒绝
- unit (police) （警察）小組、警車
- unit cost 單位成本
- unit depreciation method 單位折舊法
- unit price 单价
- unit trust 單位信託
- unity of command 統一命令
- unity of direction 統一的方向
- unity of objective 統一目標原則
- unjust 不公平,不公正,不合理,不正当
- unlawful 非法的,不合法的,违法的
- unlawful assembly 非法集會
- unlawful detention 非法拘留
- unlawful handling of 非法處理
- unlawful homicide 非法杀人

- unlawful imprisonment 非法拘禁
- unlawful possession of a weapon 非法持有
- unlawful possession 非法擁有,非法持有
- unlawful practice 非法执业
- unlawful retention 非法拘留
- unlawful sexual intercourse 非法性交
- unlawfulness 违法
- unless 除非
- unlicensed 没有执照的,没有许可证的
- unlimited company 無限公司
- unlimited liability 無限責任,無限債務責任
- unliquidated damages 未定额的损害赔偿金
- unliquidated 未清偿的
- unlisted security 未上市證券
- unloaded weapon 沒裝彈藥的槍械
- unmarked police car 便裝警車
- unnatural sex 反自然性行为,鸡奸
- unpaid dividend 未付股利
- unprecedented 前所未有的,无前例的
- unprejudiced 没有偏见的,大公无私的,公正的

- unpremeditated 无预谋的,无准备的
- unpremeditated crime 非預謀罪行
- unpresented cheque 未兑现支票
- unprofessional 不合行规的,违反专业道德的
- unquoted investment 非上市公司之投資
- unrealised profit 未實現利潤
- uphold verdict 維持原判
- unsecured 無抵押
- unsecured debt 无担保(或抵押)的债务
- unsecured loan 無擔保貸款,信用貸款
- unsettled debts 未偿付的债务
- unsettled 为偿付的,未偿清的,未决的,未定的
- unsound 不健全的,不健康的,不正常的,有瑕疵的
- unsoundness of mind 精神不健全,精神失常
- unspoken 未说出口的
- unspoken agreement 默契
- unwarranted 无保证的,无法证明为正当的
- unwarranted arrest 擅自逮捕,不当逮捕
- unwarranted charge 莫须有的罪名,无根据的控状
- unwritten 不成文的,非书面的,口头的

- unwritten convention　不成文慣例
- unwritten law　不成文法,习惯法
- upright　正直的
- up-to-date　最新的,现时的
- urgent notice　紧急通知,紧急公告
- urine test　尿液測試
- use of force　使用武力/暴力
- usurpation　篡奪、非法使用
- usury　高利貸
- utilitarianism　功利主義
- utility　效用，公共事業
- utility theft　盜竊公用設備/設施
- utmost good faith　具最高誠意絕對真確
- to utter　行使偽造物

# V

- vacancy  空缺,空间,空位
- vacancy of succession  无人继承
- vacant  空的,未被占用的,无主的,遗弃的
- vacant possession  空屋(地),空房
- vacate  搬出,撤銷
- vagrancy  流浪
- valid marriage  有效结婚
- valid, current  有效的
- validation  批准、證實、使生效
- validity of contract  合同(契约)效力
- validity  有效,效力,合法性,正当
- valuation  估值
- valuation account  計價帳戶
- valuation rule  审查规定
- valuation unit  评估单位
- value-added tax  销售税、营业税

- value-chain analysis　價值鏈分析
- vandalism　損毀行為
- variable budget　可變預算,變動性預算
- variable cost　可變成本,變動成本,非固定成本
- variable expense　變動費用
- variable overhead　變動間接製造成本
- variance analysis　差異分析
- variation　波动
- veer to the left / right　向左／右转变方向
- vehicular assault　駕車攻擊
- vehicular homicide　車禍致死
- vehicular manslaughter　駕車殺人
- vendee　買主
- vendetta　世仇
- vending machine　自動售賣機
- vendor　賣主
- venereal disease　性病
- venture capital　風險資本,創業基金
- venture　商業風險,風險企業
- venue　審判地點

- verbal    口头,言词
- verbal agreement    口頭協議
- verbal contract    口头合同/契约
- verbal error    口头上的错误,言词上的错误
- verbatim    咬文嚼字
- verdict    判决、裁决
- verifiability    可驗證性
- verification    验证,核实,证实,鉴定,确认
- vertical analysis    縱的分析
- vertical communication    縱面溝通,垂直溝通
- vertical form    垂直式
- vertical integration    縱向合併,垂直合併
- vertical merger    縱向合併
- vested rights    既定權利、應有權利
- vested    既得的,既定的,法律规定的
- veto    否决
- vexatious    无根据的,诬告的,无理取闹的,困扰的
- vexatious proceedings    滥用诉讼
- vicarious liability    替代责任,代受责任
- vice    惡性

- vice squad   警察緝捕隊
- victim   受害人,被害人,遭难者
- victim's right   受害者的權利
- victim-impact statement   被害後果陳述
- viewdata system   資料傳視系統
- vigilance   警惕、防範
- vigilante   民間警戒行劫者、民間治安維持者
- villain   惡棍
- vindication   證實無罪、證實清白
- vindictive damages   懲罰性损害赔偿金
- vindictive punishment   報復性懲罰
- to violate   违犯,违反,触犯,侵犯
- violation   違法,違規
- violence   暴力,暴行,伤害,猛烈,剧烈
- violent conduct   暴行
- violent crime   暴力犯罪
- violent offense   暴力罪行
- violent possession   暴力占有
- virtue   美德
- visible trade   有形貿易

- visitation　探親、探視,臨檢
- void　无效的,作废的
- void marriage　无效的婚姻
- voidable　可使无效的,可作废的,可撤销的
- voidable contract　可撤销的契约/合同
- voidable marriage　可宣告无效的婚姻
- voire dire　预先审查,预先查讯
- voluntary　自愿的,自动的,无偿的
- voluntary confession　出于自愿的自白,招认
- voluntary liquidation　自动清盘
- voluntary manslaughter　故意殺人
- voluntary statement　自愿供词
- vote of censure　不信任票
- voucher　傳票,憑單
- voyage policy　航程保單
- vulgarity　粗鄙
- vulnerability　弱點、易受傷害

- wage  工资
- wage rate  工資率
- wage tax classification  工资税率等级
- wage tax  工资税
- to waive  放棄
- waive rights  放棄權利
- waive time  放棄時限權利
- waiver of rights  棄權書
- wanton negligence  任意過失
- war crimes  戰爭罪行
- ward of the court  受法院監護的任
- warden  獄長
- wardship proceedings  监护权的诉讼
- warehouse  倉庫, 庫房
- warehouse warrant  倉單
- warning lights  警告燈

- warrant    法令，逮捕証，搜查證
- warrant of seizure    查封令
- warranty    保單、擔保
- warranty of legality    合法保証
- wasting asset    遞耗資產,耗竭資產
- water rights    用水權
- water transport    水上運輸
- weapon    武器,凶器
- weapon of offence 犯罪凶器,作案凶器,进攻性武器
- weaving in and out of    在行驶车辆中穿进穿出
- weight    重量,,衡量,重压,重要性
- weight of evidence    证据的份量
- weighted average    加權平均法,加權平均數
- welfare fraud    福利欺詐
- whereabouts    下落
- white supremacy    白人種族至上主義
- white-collar crime    白领罪行
- whole life insurance    終生保險單
- whole life policy    終生保險單
- wholesale banking    批發銀行業務

- wholesale co-operative society  批發合作社
- wholesale price  批發價
- wholesale trade  批發業,批發貿易
- wholesaler  批發商
- wildlife  野生動植物
- wilful default  故意不出庭,故意違約,故意拖延
- wilful misconduct  有意识的不当行为
- wilfully obstruct  故意阻挠
- will  遺囑
- winding-up  结束,结束业务
- winding-up petition  申请结束营业,申请清盘
- winding-up of business  结束营业
- winding-up of company  公司清盘,结束公司营业
- win-win situation  双赢局面
- wire tap  竊聽電話
- with prejudice  有偏見
- to withdraw  撤回、撤銷
- withdrawal  撤销,撤回,提款,退出
- within the meaning  在法律的定义内
- without cause  无故

- without discrimination 一視同仁
- without leave of 未经请准
- without prejudice 無偏見
- without reservation 无保留
- witness 目击,目睹,证人,目击者,作证,证明
- witness of the defense 辯方證人
- witness of the prosecution 控方證人
- witness stand 证人席
- work certified 證實完工程度
- work furlough 暫准監外工作
- work group 團隊組合
- work in progress 在产品
- work overtime 超時工作
- work release 工作上的假釋
- work shift 輪班
- work stoppage 停工,停工次數
- workforce 工作人口,人力資源
- working asset 營運資產
- working capital 營運資金,周轉資金,流動資本
- working capital fund 營運資金基金

- working capital management  營運資金管理
- working capital ratio  營運資金比率
- work-in-progress  在產品,在製品
- work-to-rule  按章工作
- World Trade Organization (WTO)  世界貿易組織
- wounding  伤害
- wounding with intent  蓄意伤害
- writ  令状,传票
- writ of arrest  逮捕令
- writ of detinue  交还非法扣押物令
- writ of enquiry  评定损害赔偿数额调查令
- writ of execution  执行令
- writ of fieri facias  财产扣押令
- writ of possession  归还土地与所有权人令
- writ of privilege  释放令
- writ of prohibition  禁制令
- writ of restitution  恢复物权令,归还令
- writ of right  权利令
- writ of seizure and sale  查封与拍卖令
- writ of sequestration  暂时扣押令

- writ of subpoena　传召出庭令
- writ of summons　(法庭)传票,传讯令状
- written contract　书面契约(合同)
- written down value　減記價值,減值後價值
- written judgement　书面判决,判决书
- written proof　书面证据,书面举证
- written statement　供述书,书面供词,书面陈述
- written testimony　书面证明
- written verdict　判决书,书面裁定
- wrong　错误,过失,损害,罪行,不正当的,伤害
- wrongful　违法的,非法的,不正当的,错误的
- wrongful act　不法行爲、不當行爲
- wrongful dismissal　非法解雇,非法驳回
- wrongful heir　非法的继承人

# X

- xenophile 崇洋迷外
- xenophobe 仇外
- X-rated film 色情電影

# Y

- year 年
- year-end 年末
- year-end adjustment 年終調整
- year-end dividend 年終股利
- yes / no question 是非問題
- yield method 實際利率法
- yield rate 實際獲利率
- yield ratio 實際獲利率
- yield to maturity 有效利率
- youth authority 少年罪犯管理機構
- youthful 年轻的,青年的
- youthful offender 少年犯

# Z

- zealot 狂熱、過分熱心

Notes:

DICTIONARY OF LAW    ENGLISH - CHINESE

DICTIONARY OF LAW    ENGLISH - CHINESE